DEAR GRATITUDE

AN ANTHOLOGY

CHRIS PALMORE

For Dad
It's because you chose to stay afloat during the hardest moments of both of our lives that I didn't drown.

For Mom
I am grateful for your love.

If it weren't for you, I wouldn't have life, nor would I know gratitude.

CONTENTS

FOREWORD

Every so often someone or something comes into your life that resets your focus. Rarely, however, do we know how profound these people, events, or experiences will be until we are far removed from them. They may be painful or joyful, terrifying or exhilarating, but what they all have in common is one core theme: When we look back on them, it is crystal clear that they have shaped us in ways that we needed to be shaped. They become the mile markers of our lives, defining the waypoints of our own personal journey, and yet, we likely never saw them coming, never asked or even knew to ask for them. And often they are so subtle and fleeting that we could have easily missed them if we hadn't paid attention for the split-second that they crossed our path.

That's where my own gratitude journey began about ten years ago. I can't recall exactly where I was or why I was there, but, even if I could, I don't believe it's relevant to what comes next.

"I was taking a midday walk, and as I glanced down to step off the curb and cross the street I caught a glimpse of a tiny wrinkled piece of paper not worthy of a second glance, but there was something written on it and my curiosity was piqued. I picked it up and unfolded it".

On one side of it was a short prayer to Saint Jude. On the other were four scribbled words stacked one on top of the other: Acceptance, Forgiveness, Tolerance, Gratitude.

I could contrive a wonderful narrative about how that piece of paper got there, why it came across my path, how it found me rather than my finding it, and how the universe manifests our intentions in automagical ways. In the end it just doesn't matter.

The universe isn't an Apple Watch, tracking my GPS coordinates and delivering up scraps of paper in my path like Siri reminders. I'd expect something a bit more dramatic from a universe that also produces supernovas and quasars, and regularly sucks galaxies to their death through black holes. It was a scrap of discarded paper. What matters is that I picked it up.

I held onto that little piece of paper for years and every so often I thought about the four words and wondered about the person who wrote them. Was there a sequence or a priority to the words? Was acceptance a precursor to forgiveness; tolerance required in order to be grateful? Eventually, I misplaced the tiny paper. End of story, or at least, so I thought at the time.

A few years later I wrote a short article about that experience and the importance of gratitude for a column I had in Inc Magazine. It was one of thousands of short pieces that I'd written over the years. Truth be told, it was what writers call a fluff piece, cute and touching but hardly something I thought much of. "I had a seven-article-per-month agreement with Inc and I would write about most anything to live up to that obligation."

Shortly after writing that column I had another chance encounter with gratitude.

My son had a terrible cold and I was making a midnight run to a 24-hour Walgreens to pick up cough syrup. It was mid December and snowing heavily, the kind of night you're only out driving if you have to be. As I walked into the drugstore I heard a voice from the past call my name. It was my high school wrestling coach who I hadn't seen in more than 30 years. He was a towering figure in my youth and one of those people who I knew had shaped me in ways that I can only begin to explain. Towards the end of our conversation I thanked him for having been in my life.

I wrote about that encounter in another Inc column, which was partly about what an amazing person and role model my coach had been, but mostly about how I had spent 30 years holding onto a gift that I should have delivered to him long ago; that gift was gratitude. I recounted in the column how, "I had kept my gratitude locked up inside, as though it were a museum piece, rather than giving it back to its rightful owner."

What I didn't realize at the time was that a tiny piece of paper and my seemingly insignificant act of gratitude on that December night had put into motion a cascading series of events that would turn those brief encounters with gratitude into a life-changing revelation.

A few weeks after the article was published, I received an email from Chris Palmore, who had come across my column on the recommendation of a friend. He wanted to talk about some work he was doing in establishing a non-profit focused on gratitude. I agreed to get on the phone with Chris for a short chat.

During that phone call Chris shared with me some of the stories in this book. He talked about the letter of gratitude that he wrote to his mother and his deep passion for spreading the power of gratitude to others. He was brimming with so much enthusiasm and energy that I don't recall saying more than a few words during the hour-long conversation. His enthusiasm was contagious.

I recognized, during that call, the wonderful unbridled and often naive enthusiasm of youth. Chris saw only possibilities, not obstacles—something that had driven me on my own journey. At the end of the call I asked how I could help; it was a question Chris wasn't expecting. We agreed that I'd provide a sounding board and guidance for his ideas.

Over the next few years Chris meandered through numerous attempts to spread his mission of gratitude, from a country-wide gratitude tour, to a New York City Gratitude concert, to a trip to Cuba to take his message of gratitude to the poor. His success was lackluster but his enthusiasm rarely dimmed.

During that time I tagged along, sometimes as a mentor, other times as an advisor, on a few occasions dishing out tough love, and many times simply as a friend willing to listen. I accumulated a portfolio of "Chris" stories that I often shared with friends. I was amazed at how this young man could so easily connect with people and how undaunted he was by setbacks. He was on a purpose-driven mission and nothing would dissuade him from it. His goal was simple, to reach as many people as possible with the message that gratitude can change lives.

What I didn't realize through all of this was that my own understanding of gratitude and the role it would play in my life was also changing radically.

Shortly before I met Chris, I had experienced one of the most difficult chapters in my life. In the period of a few months my mother passed away, my wife and I filed for divorce, and a business venture I'd invested heavily in hit rock bottom. There didn't seem to be much to be grateful for. I was tallying up my few misfortunes and not my many blessings.

It must serve some sort of perverse primal need that we want to wallow in our misery, perhaps in the hope that God, the universe, or some benevolent force will take enough pity on us to change our circumstances.

Yet, in-between my bouts of wallowing, I started to think about that piece of paper and every so often listing all of the things for which I needed to find acceptance, express forgiveness, learn to be tolerant of, and lastly, the nearly endless list of the people and things I was grateful for. That practice became a daily morning ritual that still starts my day. Being grateful didn't somehow bring me everything I desired, but it amplified my appreciation for all that I had.

Nothing is harder when you are in the darkest corners of your life than choosing to be grateful, and yet, in those moments, absolutely nothing is more important, more healing, more affirming, and more comforting than the simple act of expressing gratitude. Reading through the anthology of letters in this book reveals just how universal that truth is. But it also reveals something even more profound—that at any moment it is our choice to be grateful; even in the darkest moments of our lives we can choose to refocus our attention on the myriad ways in which we are each blessed. We can look back on some of the most painful times and still be grateful for how they delivered us to where we are. We can regret what we've lost or we can cherish what we still have.

That choice is not always an easy or obvious one. Which is why, as with any habit, gratitude needs to be practiced, it has to become part of what you do on your worst days and on your best days; you need to remind yourself daily of what you are grateful for and, most importantly, you have to share the gift of gratitude with those to whom it ultimately belongs, the people you are grateful for.

Reading this book, and the many stories of gratitude from others who have also chosen to do just that, will help you to create that habit, to better understand the power of gratitude, and to reaffirm its ability to heal your own wounds and to bring you to a place of peace and joy.

Ultimately, the message of this book, and the many people who contributed to it, is that gratitude is a choice, and, like that tiny tattered scrap of paper that was blown into my path by forces unforeseen and unknown, this book has also been placed on your path. I'll let you make up your own reasons for how and why that happened now, at this precise moment in your life.

But, in the end, all that really matters is that you picked it up, and by doing so you've chosen gratitude.

T. Koulopoulos - Boston 2020

DEAR GRATITUDE

Dear Gratitude,

It took me forty-one years to write to you. Better late than never.

I didn't really know about you till a few years back. The true revelation of your presence in my life came from a place of loss. Is it true we don't really appreciate the things we have until they are gone? I can tell you in this moment with all of my heart that I choose not to live that way. I want to appreciate all the things and people now. I don't want to live with regret. I want to live in love.

I didn't know it at the time but you were there when I was born. I can recount the story my mom told me of my birth. She had lost who would have been my older brother a year or so before because of a premature birth. This time around, her new doctor made the call to have her sewed up so that I would arrive at the appropriate time. My mom chose to have stitches put in her body before I was even born. That's how much she wanted me to be in this world. I know that she had immense gratitude for the doctor's decision as I am now grateful for the choices that were made only from the experience of true loss my parents had. They chose to spin the wheel again because they wanted a boy. I write this happy and healthy, forty-one years later, with a little wear and tear.

You were there when my heart was broken. You were there when I felt alone. You were there when I was disappointed. I didn't know it at the time but the lesson which took many repetitions was learned: You have always been present. I can honestly look back and say that I am grateful for all the sad moments of my life. I wouldn't change those memories or moments for I am who I am because of them.

You have allowed me to see all the love in my life and appreciate all the things that continue to work in my favor. When something doesn't go according to plan, I remember you are present. When anger or hurt bangs on my door, I know that at a moment's notice I can run into your arms. I thought this year I would get everything I wanted. Now I know this year is the year I get to appreciate everything I have.

I know that if I start each day thanking you for the air I breathe and for a heart that keeps beating, I will be ready for whatever comes my way. I strive to keep you always close and within my thoughts. I have all that I need and so much more. This is the way it has always been.

Thank you for being patient with this hard-headed student. I've always felt loved, but it took the acknowledgement of your presence for me to love myself.

Chris Palmore - September 25th, 2020

ARE YOU LISTENING?

Words float around us all day long. Some we hear, and others we completely ignore. We are often in our own world dealing with our own thoughts, and many words are often just noise, white noise, regardless of whether they are interesting or not. We never know when we are going to be present enough to hear something that we choose to actively listen to, then realize it resonates with us enough to put it into practice.

In 2013, I helped my friend Corey drive from Louisville, Kentucky, to his new home in San Francisco. One of the last nights I was there, Corey and I went to Cobb's Comedy Club, a historic comedy club where all the greats have played, to see Adam Carolla doing his stand up routine. The place was packed.

Adam shared his story, with pictures, of his rise from rags to comfortable circumstances to eventual riches with humility and humor. It was really a motivational talk with comedy fully mixed into it. He mentioned his podcast, The Adam Carolla Show, at a time when podcasts were fairly new, and I made a mental note to look into it.

Soon after, I started listening to Adam's podcast regularly. He had a new one five days a week, Monday through Friday. They ranged from ninety minutes to two hours. I walked around the house going through my morning routine with my earbuds on, listening to Adam who brought the comedy but also shared some words of wisdom.

GIVING GRATITUDE

It was sometime in October or November when he said something that changed my life. He was talking about his birthday and about how he never celebrated it. At first, it had to do with his parents not caring enough, but eventually it became something entirely different. He felt that a birthday was life's version of a participation trophy. A participation trophy means nothing if everyone gets one. There is no value to it. It made sense to me. What I understood was we should give thanks to someone in our life on this day, someone to whom our birthday means something. What if, on our birthday, we gave gifts or cards to those we loved most thanking them for how they made our life better in the past year? What if, instead of being a receiver, we chose to be a giver on that day? We could celebrate our appreciation for that person by expressing our gratitude.

What exactly is gratitude? Webster defines "gratitude" as *the state of being grateful* and *thankfulness.* So what is grateful? Webster's definition of "grateful" is *appreciative of benefits received, expressing gratitude and thanks.* This is the definition we find in dictionaries, but like all abstract words, "gratitude" must be felt to be understood.

To quote my mentor and friend, Thomas Koulopoulos:

"We talk about it all the time; we all know the word. We know the definition of gratitude, but I'm not sure we get it if we haven't truly experienced it. Once you get gratitude, there is this aha moment, when you realize it's not just about thanking someone. It's about why you weren't already thanking them. What was standing in the way? What kind of deep-rooted issue did you have that created an obstacle to sharing that gratitude? If you answer that question honestly, then you'll get gratitude. You'll understand what it was about you that was flawed, that was broken, that was wounded, that prevented you from expressing your gratitude. Whatever it is that stands in the way is what you need to figure it out. Gratitude is a path to understanding and accepting yourself and your own power. Only then can you experience gratitude and share its benefits with others."

Thomas Koulopoulos

Unfortunately, as humans, we like to complicate what is truly simple. We overthink and choose not to take action. This non-start is a reason a lot of people won't ever experience the true power of gratitude. The mind is amazing. At any given moment, we have the ability to choose what to focus on and determine what it all means. Our thoughts form our ideas and these ideas create the world we see.

If gratitude was "the path to figuring that out," gratitude was exactly what I was experiencing then. Why wasn't I expressing my thanks then?

My birthday was close, and I wanted it to be about someone else. I wanted to celebrate my mother. I didn't, at the time, know how I was going to do this, but the thought was there.

MY BIRTHDAY

My gift for my thirty-fifth birthday was a message I posted on my mom's Facebook wall. I did this for two reasons: First, I wanted her to find it and be surprised. Second, I wanted it to be public. This is what I posted:

December 30th, 2013 - My 35th Birthday

Dear Mom,

I turned 35 today and this question has been floating around in my head the last few days: I'm all for celebrating with others, don't get me wrong, but could there be a better way to celebrate my birthday?

If I'm being totally honest with you, I didn't really do anything on December 30th, 35 years ago. I truly have no memory of it.

Now if you ask my mom, I'm sure she could tell you and convey a strong emotion with the events leading up to and including my birth. Is this day mine, really, to celebrate? Is living out another 365 days worth celebrating?

I'm not suggesting not celebrating the day of your birth, I'm suggesting that you celebrate your mom on your birthday. There are many reasons for this train of thought. Here are two: first, we have no memory or any true action on our part surrounding the event; second, as much as we enjoy receiving gratitude, giving true gratitude is a much healthier and fulfilling action.

I have no problem admitting that I'm selfish. I believe that there are selfish acts that a person can perform that are truly wonderful. When thanking someone, the giver is the one that benefits. I'd like to repeat that.

When being kind to another, the giver is the one that truly benefits. You can't feel what the other person is feeling. What you feel is the vibe you get from how you make them feel.

Now I know that I'm not the first person to think of this. I just wanted to tell my mom that I love her, that I appreciate the pain, suffering, and self-sacrifice she has endured on my behalf not only on the day of my birth but also for the years that followed, that I am fully aware that I wasn't always the easiest person to love, but she always made me feel loved. I just wanted to tell her all this on my birthday.

Mom, I pledge this coming year to tell you that I love you more often, and I will find more ways to let you know how special you are to me and make you prouder.

Love always,
Chris

I knew that my mom would call me and let me know she had read the letter. But time passed and I didn't receive a call. This was strange because normally my parents would give me a call together on the morning of my birthday. They would sing happy birthday and tell me they loved me. I was expecting at least this much, but no call came.

By mid-morning I decided to call my dad. I didn't call my mom because I was still hoping to surprise her. Dad answered, saying "happy birthday" with a smile in his voice.

I thanked him and quickly pivoted the conversation to Mom. I asked him if she had read the letter. He said that she had and that she couldn't talk to me right then. He said, "She was so moved by it that she needed time to process it all. She was speechless."

That left *me* speechless. The relationship I had with my mom had always been very close; we talked almost daily. From a young age, I had no problem saying I love you and giving her a kiss on the cheek in public.

That at this moment I had rendered her with no voice with just my words on a computer screen, still to this day, amazes me. That's the true power of showing gratitude.

The letter strengthened our relationship. It ended up having a lot of likes and comments. It was addressed to the public, so it allowed others to share it. The love that came out of others was magical, and it happened only because I got the ball rolling. Gratitude breeds gratitude.

I could never have known that four months to the day later, on April 30th, Mom would be gone.

WHY ANOTHER BOOK ON GRATITUDE?

Society has become divided on so many levels that we sometimes forget all that unites us. We all experience joy and pain, we all mourn our losses and celebrate our victories, we all have beliefs and philosophies, we all hope to be healthy, we all know fear, and we all have a lot to be grateful for. We are all truly one in gratitude.

I went through a tremendous loss which changed my life because of a single act of sharing gratitude. That's the story of how this book came to be. Books are similar to ideas in how they float around and can land anywhere. Many wonderful books have been written about gratitude, so, why one more? Why or how this book got in your hands really tickles the curiosity place in my brain. Chances are that it was the result of some sequence of serendipitous events. Whatever the reason, one thing is clear: You're making a conscious choice to think about how gratitude will impact your life. Perhaps your life is going well and you want to share your good fortune, or perhaps you are in a dark place and you're wondering what to be grateful for. The thing about gratitude is that it can exist in both of these cases and all the ones in between.

In his book *The Life-Changing Power of Gratitude*, Marc Reklau has a chapter titled "Is It All Good, Even the Bad Stuff?" in which he shares a parable about twin brothers whose father was a raging alcoholic.

This man abused his kids in ways that just wouldn't be appropriate for a book with the word gratitude in its title. Just suffice it to say that their childhood was horrible. Years later, when the boys had become adults, their father died and there was no love lost. One of the brothers, a massively successful businessman, was loved throughout their town. People were happy to see him walk down the street and he helped whomever he could. He loved life and gave back in multiple ways. His brother, on the other hand, having followed in his father's footsteps, was abusive to those around him and mean to anyone that crossed his path.

One day, the family doctor was called on to check up on the

businessman. The doctor, having not seen him since he was a child and having known his father, asked him how he had become so successful.

"Doctor you know how... You knew my father," the businessman replied.

The same doctor, a year or so later, was called to visit the other brother. Once he arrived at the place, he noticed it had cracked windows and a leaky ceiling. He could feel the anger and negative vibes in the air. The doctor looked at the twin and asked him how it had come to this, why he and his house were such a disaster?

The second twin, without any hesitation, said, "Doctor you know how... You knew my father."

Perspective is one of the keys to unlocking a grateful heart. Two people can have the same experience and choose to react in different ways. This is a superpower that was given to you at birth. I know that it's possible that you never knew you had it, but you do. At any given moment, you get to decide what it all means to you. At any given moment, like my friend Deano Sutter said on my podcast, you can be a hero or you can be a victim. You can be the first brother or you can be the second brother.

If you only walk away with the knowledge that you hold the power to be grateful, I will consider this book a massive success.

We all have personal hardships, dark moments when all seems lost. We also have a choice. We can let these challenges destroy us or we can control how they make us feel, how they affect us. Extreme actions deserve extreme thinking, and we have the gift to decide how to react to our hardships. We can decide to look at the struggles through the lens of gratitude. We can choose to use our gratitude as an anchor to get us through the storm.

In all of these cases, the key word is *decide*. As my friend Bobby Kountz said in his book *The Someday Solution*, "When we decide, we are saying to ourselves that we will persist no matter what. When we decide, we commit. When we commit, we win, eventually. The combination of patience, belief, persistence, and the ability to decide is unstoppable!" Once we make that decision and commit to being grateful, we're engaged.

It's impossible to hold a positive and negative thought in the mind at once, so when we turn to our gratitude, we can dissolve that negative thinking. It takes practice to make gratitude a reflex, and, in times of struggle, it is a superpower, but the result will make us both stronger and healthier.

If you are part of the crowd that has already experienced the true meaning of gratitude, this book will easily flow into your daily practice. I recommend reading an essay or letter a day, but feel free to jump around. Reading this book might inspire you to ask another person what or whom they are grateful for, discover how grateful you are for something you've always taken for granted, or even write a gratitude letter yourself.

For those that struggle with gratitude, this book can be a tool for self-exploration and reflection. It can help you find answers about what you're truly grateful for and whether or not you might feel comfortable sharing your gratitude.

If you've never tried expressing it before, it's easy. There's plenty to be grateful for.

Just look around you. You can find ten things the first minute, but start with just three. Is there a cup, a bed, a chair, some clothes, a toothbrush, soap, a book, a pen, or a phone around you? Do you have access to it? Do you use it? Find the first three things you see that you use daily. Make a note of these things. Be thankful you have these three things. Write them down. Then think about all the ways you use these. Appreciate them again. Express your gratitude by either saying it out loud or writing it down. "I'm grateful for my ----
-. Without it, I wouldn't be able to -----."

Many have shared their gratitude in this book. My hope is that some of the stories will resonate with you, that the lights will come on, that you will get to a place where practicing gratitude makes sense not only in the good times, but also in the bad. I hope, by reading this book, you will be tuning your brain daily to the idea of gratitude. I hope you create your own gratitude space. I hope you create love daily, in your life as well as in others'. I hope you initiate gratitude and share it.

Through this process, the process of hearing and reading others' gratitude, I have continued to learn and find new things to be grateful for and new ways to be grateful. This mirror reflection that occurs through the experiences of someone other than yourself is a gift. It has forever changed my life, and I'm grateful for it.

There are many different flavors of gratitude to choose from. What if gratitude is like ice cream? Some like plain vanilla, others like exotic flavors, some like toppings,... What I'm simply saying is that gratitude is personal. It means something different to everyone. This book's goal is to expose you to as many different flavors and varieties of gratitude as possible so you can create your very own "gratitude sundae" if you will. What's your favorite flavor of gratitude?

MY MOTHER

Her cancer came back and wouldn't take no for an answer. My superhero of a mother became so swollen from cancer that the doctors had to drain her lungs to allow her to breathe, and she was in so much pain that she had to take as much medication as she had treatments just to get by.

Dr. Williams, my mom's doctor, cared for her with honesty and grace for years, and there was no better person to hold her hand as she heard the news that, medically, they couldn't do any more.

Once my mom knew there was no hope for her to recover, she made the decision to come home for what became the last week of her life. There are good memories here.

She would spend as much time as possible on the screen porch. The weather was nice and I remember a day when many people came to just sit and be with her. It was wonderful. She was so happy and grateful to them, and I was too. We got my mom out in her wheelchair because at this time it wasn't possible for her to walk very far on her own and she had become oxygen dependent just to breathe.

There were fifteen or more of us and we walked as my dad pushed her down to the park. She loved walks and being outside and we did this all together. It really was a wonderful moment and my mom was herself in this moment, smiling like she always had on our walks together.

In the end, the in-home hospice nurse had to call her an ambulance. By this time, my mom was in much pain and had to take liquid morphine. The last memory I have of my mom being conscious is of the paramedics wheeling her toward the backdoor.

They stopped for a moment and I kissed her on the cheek. She didn't know what was going on and asked what was happening. Then they wheeled her out as I stayed right where I was. I didn't have the strength to watch them put her in the ambulance.

She was put into a medically induced coma once she was

admitted and within eighteen hours died in the middle of the night as my dad lay on a mattress on the floor next to her.

Because of Adam Carolla, I got to spend the last four months of my mother's life showing gratitude to her. Because of Adam Carolla, I wrote that letter to her before she died instead of after she was already gone. I was grateful for Adam. A comedian whose podcast I had listened to had inspired my gratitude journey.

"To quote Monty Python, 'you're not dead yet.' We don't mourn the living."

Doctor Patrick Williams

WORDS OF WISDOM

by Richard Calautti

Richard Calautti, residing in Perth, Australia, is the founder of Live Life Now Project.

There's a wealth of wisdom about life that cancer patients and survivors can teach us about gratitude and the important, simple things in life that we take for granted on a daily basis. We get so caught up in daily trivial matters without realising that things could be so much worse. We fail to notice simply being alive and recognising how lucky us "well" individuals are can be a gift in itself.

I started interviewing cancer patients about the important things in life in 2009, following a period living in London surrounded by people who were stressed, busy, exhausted and seemingly running around in circles trying to make as much money as possible, yet not particularly happy or satisfied with life. I was one of these people.

I had always conducted my own survey research around various topics, but I was really looking for something deeper, more compelling and life affirming. I wanted to be reminded of what was really important in life, aside from what I was frantically chasing to make me "happy."

I'd read self-help books for comfort and guidance but was searching for advice from actual, real people rather than the opinion of a psychologist who, for example, had written text from years of research. I decided to ask advice from people who had "faced" death yet had the opportunity to review their life and consider how they may have lived differently, believing there was some wisdom to be gained through these life-changing circumstances.

This led me to survey cancer patients on a number of topics as a way of helping "well" individuals like myself to realise that our daily struggles were minor and trivial compared to a potentially life-threatening illness. My theory was that a cancer diagnosis must really put the important things in life into focus and provide an insight into life, and that those of us "stressed" about our comparatively minor daily dramas had forgotten how lucky we were to be healthy and alive.

The survey questions were initially completed locally in Perth, Australia, via a cancer support organisation, and have grown internationally since I started a page on Instagram in April 2015 with quotes from patients around the world. Gratitude about life comes through strongly in many of these quotes. The quick, easily-read quotes resonated deeply with people on many levels throughout the world.

Patients and healthy individuals responded to these insights, commenting on the difference they'd made to their lives, proving that the human experience and human struggles are universal.

Each quote reflects the patient's personal story, and there's so much that those of us living normal, healthy lives can learn about how lucky we are to have the struggles we have. Simply waking up each day and being grateful for the "healthy" life we have is a gift. Recognising this fact also makes a positive impact on our life.

The cancer patients and survivors who contribute quotes to my project are real, human, living examples of gratitude, hope, courage and inner strength. Their wisdom was gained from insurmountable pain and fearful circumstances. Yet, through all of this, they teach us enormous lessons around how grateful we should be to face another day and be thankful for our simple blessings. They provide an appreciation of the real treasures of life and the importance of love, family, friends, self-belief, gratitude, resilience, and never giving up. They so clearly remind us "well" individuals of what really is important in life. They are an invaluable source of hope and courage.

There's no doubt that a cancer diagnosis can be truly devastating. And every single one of us has been affected by cancer in some way. Cancer patients who have contributed to this project have helped people who suffer mental illness, depression, loneliness, and relationship breakdowns or people simply having a bad day and needing some comfort and guidance.

Looking at life through the eyes of someone who has faced death is one of the clearest ways to realise how grateful we are to have another day, whether that is to experience the "daily grind," sit in traffic, or even have the luxury of complaining about the minor and, ultimately, utterly meaningless things to which we devote so much time and energy. For all of it, we should be grateful. It could be a lot worse.

Many participants in the research have since lost their battle to cancer, yet their quotes live on and are a source of hope, courage and inspiration to others facing their own personal struggles, enabling them to truly live life now and recognise the importance that gratitude for one's daily blessings, no matter how small, really is one of life's greatest treasures.

For the cancer patients and survivors who have contributed to my project in a way that helps me and others realise what's important in life, I express my utmost gratitude.

To "well" individuals who are able to reflect on this advice, look at their own lives, and make positive changes to their lives and the lives of those around them, I am grateful.

I started this project as a way of helping myself find some meaning in life. I am grateful for all contributors and followers who keep this project alive.

EARLIEST MEMORIES

"With praise and thanksgiving they sang to the Lord" Ezra 3:11

Some of my earliest memories of my mom involve her reading to me while I was in the bathtub. She had this picture book of Bible stories and would read it to me while I was soaking in the tub. Many may listen to an audiobook while being in the tub, but someone reading to you, that's a mother and son thing. Good memories.

My mom loved to sing. I grew up in a house where singing was always present. It wasn't till years later when I learned to play the guitar that I learned to love to sing. My mom was in the choir at church and played the piano. She had a piano teacher come a few times to give me lessons. I didn't show any interest and that was that. In this instance, I wish she would have made me take lessons for a little longer to see if I could have been hooked. Who knows? It could have been the wrong teaching method, just me, or the wrong timing.

When I got older, we once visited my grandparents for the holidays, as we usually did, and my grandfather picked up an organ. I remember seeing him play. The instrument was fascinating, so many buttons and two different levels of keys. It was an expensive organ. There was a place by our house that taught elderly people how to play the organ for free. The catch was that they sold organs. Give a little, get more. My grandfather thought it sounded like a great place to go and learn with other people his age. I like how active he was in his late years. It was like he never slowed down until his body made him.

Another fond memory of my mother is how she would wake me up in the morning. She would come into my room, open the shades, and say in a loud jovial voice, "Rise and shine and give God the glory." That was my mom; she had the most wonderful smile and presence. If a person could be a home for another person, this is what my mom was to me. My mom was my home. I was my mother's son, and my sister was my dad's daughter, just different personality traits. Mine was the love of the arts, music, acting, and creating. These were from my mom. I feel my writing in this moment is from her, and I can imagine her cheering me on with every day of writing.

There are a few similarities between my mom and me. My mom lost her mom to cancer at a young age. She also had breast cancer. I was a little older when I lost her than my mom was when she lost hers. At the time she lost her mom, my mom was married and had two children; I was married and had two step sons when I lost my mom. The important thing is that I wasn't alone at home with the stress, heartache, and loss of my mother.

I still don't know how my dad does it. I know that it was the hardest on him and will forever be. She was my mom, but to him, she was his life, his partner in adventure. They were very different people, but they loved each other and showed me what love was. They were my image of a loving relationship. They weren't perfect. Maybe that's just because I was a momma's boy and my memories fall back on seeing him ask for forgiveness with an open and honest heart. I know that my mom wasn't perfect; no one is. But I honestly can't think or have a memory of her being mean or hurtful ever to anyone. She cared for me and others, many others. She was a caregiver and I was fortunate to be her son.

DEATH AND DEPRESSION

"A life of service is a life well and greatly lived."
Omoakhuana Anthonia

The week after my mom's death is all a blur. I thought of that letter I had written to her and it made me feel sad. I had written I would tell her I love her more this year and spend more time with her. That was it. There was no more time, ever. This became part of my despair. I wasn't ready to see the positivity in it, or how it could bring light into this darkness.

We weren't going to have an open casket. I know my mom would have agreed with it. There were going to be a lot of people coming up to talk and share stories about my mom. I wasn't in any position to want to speak in front of a crowd during this time, especially with my mom's body in the room. After giving it a lot of thought, I decided that what I wanted to share was the letter I wrote to my mom on my last birthday.

My thirty-fifth birthday became very special to me. I had done something I had never done before, and it had connected my mother and me in an unforgettable way. I just wanted to honor her on my birthday and let her know that I loved her and cared for her more than words could describe. It was a simple message from the heart with action steps moving forward in the year.

I had my cousin read that note at her funeral. A lot of the people at the funeral had already read it on Facebook months before. What mattered was I wanted to say goodbye to my mom with a sentiment of gratitude, and I silently did this as my cousin spoke for me on this day.

I really do believe that my mom would have been happy with her funeral. It was a celebration of her. She never would have wanted it to be a sad occasion. My mom's life was a joyous, loving adventure. Many people shared stories. People laughed and cried. We even had balloons.

The rest of that year was really hard as depression settled in and gained residency in my life. I would think of the letter and those traumatic experiences leading up to my mom's death that were overshadowing the years and years of good and happy memories. I was angry, really angry, and in free fall. But I knew that every day that passed was distancing me from the trauma, and my head was clearing up a little bit at a time. It was as if I were coming up for oxygen while being lost at sea.

Love Never Dies
"The song has ended but the melody lingers on..."
Irving Berlin

DEAR DAD

Come the following December I decided to write a letter to my dad. I had come to look at my dad differently this past year. I knew that the pain I had felt for the loss was only a fraction of what he was going through. One of the most traumatic moments leading up to my mom's death was when her doctor told him, in private, the end was definite. The way my dad fell to his knees, the pain, the crying, the pleading, and the nurses who came in to help him so that he didn't have a cardiac episode and have to be hospitalized made me realize she was his life. The fact that he was still moving around, getting up, and being active was a true testament to my dad's strength and ability to love. He really is my hero, and, in my life, there will never be a person who will love me and help me in the ways he has. He is that guy and owns that spot. No one could ever take it from him. For me, in this life, he's it.

I posted the letter to my dad on the website I was working on at the time. I wanted it to stay visible and not get pushed back by newer posts like it would on Facebook. The effect of this letter was similar to that of the first one. It caused my dad to take pause and feel my love, and it made our relationship stronger. It's worth the time to sit and think and write these letters of gratitude.

In the coming months, I decided I wanted to encourage others to have the same experience I had with my letters. It was just a nugget of an idea and made me ask myself *How can I do that?* I started going to Starbucks and working on a website that would allow this to happen. I designed and wrote the website and, in the process, met amazing people who gave great advice and encouragement. It was months in the making, but having my best friend Corey's wife, Kate, who had a birthday the following week write a letter was the correct time to launch the website I had started.

INGRATITUDE IS UGLY

"There is nothing worse for the lying soul than the mirror of reality."
Steve Maraboli

Long ago, I was taught an important lesson. It was a hard lesson, and fortunately my dad was ready for this to happen. I'm not saying he was expecting it, but he had the insight and soundness of mind to show me the way.

It was, I believe, my tenth birthday. My parents threw me a little party. I was sitting at the head of the table, opposite the windows facing our backyard. My dad had set up the camcorder that he had borrowed from the school where he taught. They happily sang happy birthday to me.

Once the singing ended, I blew out the candles. A little later, I opened my presents, mostly clothes and things I was not impressed by or even happy to get. I was frowning the whole time, the lack of happiness plastered all over my face.

People who loved me had spent time and money celebrating me, all to make me feel special and loved, but this was totally lost on me at this young age in my life. I was a selfish child who just wanted toys. My dad was video recording my birthday celebration. I don't remember this moment at all. I remember what happened after this moment, later in the day.

My dad told me to go into our television room and sit down. He then played the video of me during the party. I could see how I was acting. I could see my ingratitude. I could see the ugliness it radiated. My dad explained to me how mean I was being. He explained it and showed it to me. This created a memory I will never forget. Modern technology allows a person, in this case a parent and a child, to revisit an event with the slightest of ease.

Seeing yourself behave awfully is a powerful lesson. It's hard to watch and it takes a special person, a person who cares, to show it to you. My dad showed me a lot of love, tough love. I deserved to be punished, but, instead, he cared enough to show me the ugliness so that I could see the truth of the situation and make a choice not to be that person ever again.

"Beauty is only skin deep, but ugly goes clean to the bone."

Dorothy Parker

The sooner we can understand and see all the gifts around us, the better. To be receiving so much and not taking notice of it is a disease. It will rot you from within and steal your joy. This disease silences happiness. It breaks up families and friendships. All people want is to feel appreciated and loved. Giving appreciation freely will result in it being freely given back to you. It's reciprocal, and it works. Spin the wheel, and it will come back around to you.

THE FAN

by Farhana

Farhana is a medical doctor with over ten years of experience, a wellbeing expert specialising in the practise of gratitude, and a co-creator of Gratitube, a unique video gratitude journaling app.

As we settle into the middle of September, I'm starting to feel a little nostalgic already about recent hot summer days spent horizontal in the park, dining al fresco on the balcony, and that soul charging feeling of the mighty sun on my skin.

In my nostalgic haze, I look around my room and a particular object grabs my attention and widens my smile. It's not an object you may recognise in terms of its purpose. It's not an object that is worth anything in monetary terms. It's not an object that fits in to the minimalist, gold and black themed bedroom of a thirty-something old woman; in fact, you could mistake it for garbage.

I'm referring to a customised, hand held fan made out of cardboard which was created for me on one of the hottest days this summer by two of my favourite people, my niece and nephew. The fan is folded with precision by its five- and seven-year-old creators and covered with vibrant felt pen images of things that I hold dear including a soccer ball, the outdoors, and, of course, the three of us hanging out together.

We were sweltering on the day they made this for me, and, seeing beads of sweat pour down my face after a session of playing goalkeeper whilst they kicked balls at me, they took it upon themselves to get crafty and make me this fan. Their artistic talent and neon colours aside, the best bit was that it worked and they took it in turns to fan my face for a good five minutes to help to cool me down. I felt so grateful in that moment to have such a considerate, kind and creative niece and nephew.

Since the days they were born, every time I'm with them, I feel overwhelmed by how fortunate I am to be their aunt. I couldn't appreciate how much love I could have for these two until they came into my life.

Sometimes I wish I could pause the getting older process for them so that they can stay as the perfect and cute selves that they are today. But then they grow anyway, and somehow become even more perfect and cute, and I feel enormous joy in seeing them evolve.

Whenever I'm stressed or a little sad, spending time with them is a perfect antidote, the most privileged distraction one can find. Despite having more than thirty years between us, we are simply best friends.

It's the simple things we are often grateful for. I've kept this fan and will hold on to it until next summer. When the temperature hits 30 degrees Celsius again, I'll be ever grateful for this folded, illustrated scrap of card.

NEXT STOP: A MONASTERY

"A mind that is stretched by a new experience can never go back to its old dimensions."

Oliver Wendell Holmes

Have you ever cried without knowing why? This has happened to me once in my life. It was at the Abbey of Gethsemani Monastery in Bardstown, Kentucky. A few weeks earlier, while talking with my good friend Rick, I had mentioned to him how I wanted to get away from it all for a few days, go somewhere remote and really be alone. I had looked at cabins, but they were far away or too expensive. He asked if I knew the monastery in Bardstown, an hour away from me. I didn't. He said they allowed people to stay overnight.

I was surprised to hear there were monks and a monastery so close to my home and I could go and stay there. I immediately went to their website and read up about the place. It was over a hundred years old and in a remote place in Bardstown, Kentucky. They hosted personal and group retreats. They only asked for a donation. So I emailed a monk, explained I wanted to visit, and asked how soon I could go.

All of this was happening when I was dreaming up my first gratitude-based site and the idea of people writing gratitude letters to others on the site and sharing them with me and the world. I had asked Kate, my best friend's wife, whose birthday was coming up, to write a gratitude letter on her birthday. The website was set to launch at the same time I was going to be at this monastery.

The day I was set to travel to the monastery, a blizzard hit, which is not normal in Kentucky, but I was stoic and said snow and ice wasn't going to stop me. What would have normally taken forty-five minutes took two hours, but it was fine. I had gotten up silly early and was excited about my weekend adventure into solitude in a holy place.

When I arrived, I was overwhelmed by the dramatic feel the place had. It was like in a movie, similar to castle-like buildings, old stone buildings. There was snow everywhere, and everything was quiet all around, a vast expanse all draped in white and no one to be found. Picture Jack Nicholson arriving at The Stanley Hotel. I made my way inside and rang a little bell. A monk appeared. He was very kind and explained the rules and showed me to my room. It was a good-sized room with bare brick walls with a private bathroom.

I made the decision, after I talked with the monk, that this was going to be a silent retreat for me, my first and last since, not because it wasn't pleasant; I just haven't been in the correct setting to make it happen again.

The place was amazing and, because of the blizzard, I basically had it all to myself. Everyone else that was set to be there on retreat had not shown up because of the weather. The place was really quiet and eerily peaceful, like no other place I had ever been.

That first day I got settled. The monks would meet every four hours in the chapel, sing, and have a little service. My sleeping schedule was pretty crazy during these times and this wasn't an issue at all. There was an upper seating area high above the main floor and I would go up there. I could peer in and have a bird's eye view. I felt a part of it all but from a distance and there was no one else up there. I walked all over the place, checked out the library, and found a meditation room on the top floor of one of the buildings that seemed completely empty. The view overlooked the hillside and forest that was blanketed in white.

The next morning I was sitting in my bed with my computer, and Kate's gratitude letter came through. I took a breath and read it.

KATE'S LETTER

THINKING OF YOU ON MY BIRTHDAY

Dear Mom and Dad,

Happy birthday to me! Woohoo! I made it to 30! That thought makes me smile, grimace and shudder simultaneously. I am making a conscious effort not to grimace too much, however, as wrinkles are not something I just read about in books anymore. These well-earned lines on my face convey I've been here for a little while now and I've experienced a great deal of excitement! I've often been told I don't have a good poker face. 30. Thirty. THərdē/. I am thirty, happy and healthy. I have terrific friends who remain constant despite miles of distance between us. My wonderful, adventurous husband keeps life's remarkable wheels spinning wildly beneath my feet, and yet always catches me when I get tripped up. My energetic, animated daughter has taught me to love more deeply and passionately than I ever imagined possible. And I have a crazy, snarly puppy that would give his left nut for just 5 minutes of playing fetch.

How did I get here, to this point? Well we most certainly need not get into the nitty gritty details, but I am immensely grateful that you two loved each other so very much on that special night about 30 years and 10 months ago – give or take. If it weren't for that precise moment there would be no ME! That, however, is only a mere speckle of the story. Nature + nurture. So I was born and then you raised me. Mom, you taught me to be strong and independent, to stand tall with my shoulders back (or else you would dig your freaking knuckles into my spinal column)! Dad, you taught me how to think outside of the box, how to resolve puzzles when pieces are missing, and how to "MacGyver" anything. Your mutual support of my endeavors in school, athletics, and my career is something I cherish always and will excitedly pass on to my children. You taught me that my best is always good enough. Your empowering trust has driven me to work hard and give my all in life. My life is great because of this, because of you.

You raised me to be tough, to laugh, to tell a joke and to take a joke. You taught me sarcasm in all its glory. You taught me how to fight, and then how to apologize and forgive. You taught me to respect my elders and be kind to my neighbors. *You taught me to be honest and just. You taught the good and the bad. You showed me life in its most beautiful, vulnerable and dreadful states. You welcomed sick relatives in to live with us, knowing they would breathe their last breaths in our home. You comforted and cared for them during their last days, helping them find peace in those trying moments. Through these and your multitude of selfless actions over the years, you taught me empathy and understanding, generosity and compassion. You taught me to feel sadness and despair, and to grow through these raw emotions. You taught me to be grateful for my life and all that I have in this moment. You taught me to truly live, to feel alive. No matter how challenging some moments may seem, I know how to find the good in life and that it is never too far away. You taught me this. I am so very lucky to be alive... to be 30... to be your daughter. I love you two more than you will ever know because words and actions cannot display my heart's story. I am thankful for you always. I am proud to call you Mom and Dad and I will do the best I can in life. I hope this proves you did the best you could raising me.*

Thanks for giving me thirty birthdays. I look forward to thirty-one.

I love you,
Katie Kates

∾

It was beautiful and I was crying. But I wasn't crying because it was beautiful.... I knew that feeling and it wasn't this. This was a new feeling entirely. I didn't know what was happening. I was crying completely caught up in an emotion and I didn't know what it was. I didn't know what was happening.

After searching myself for some time, I figured out what was happening. This letter I was reading on my computer, this letter of love, appreciation, and gratitude, solely existed in the physical world because I'd asked Kate to write it. Kate had these feelings inside of her. She expressed herself by writing them down, and all I had done was ask her to write a letter and share it with me... and the world.

This changed my life. I have never been the same since. I will be forever changed, knowing the power of asking another to share love in this form that can be shared and viewed by all.

GRATITUDE SQUARED

THE BIGGEST LESSON

by Catherine Robertson

The biggest lesson I ever learned happened without warning during an ordinary workday.

The manager of our sales team had been participating in an intense year-long leadership course, and, throughout that time, we had witnessed some big changes in his management style. He had become more vulnerable, self-aware, open, calm, and balanced in a way that he hadn't been before. So intrigued were we by his transformation that we invited the 'leadership guru' responsible to present at our next team meeting.

Our workload at the time was exceptionally heavy, so we were eager and willing to learn as much as we could about how to decrease stress levels and manage our time better. We met Michael Bunting that day with a high degree of expectation that he would be able to help solve all our problems.

Sitting with our pen and notepads poised, we listened to our speaker who began by admitting he had no presentation slides to show us, no specific content prepared, and would be practicing mindfulness by tuning into the moment and speaking to us from his heart.

We all nervously laughed, somewhat confused as this was not the typical way our corporate training sessions ran. No one who had presented to us before had ever mentioned mindfulness or of having a connection to their heart. It all felt a little unusual, and I remember feeling some apprehension wondering what was coming next. Michael then asked us to turn to the person seated next to us and to list all the factors in our life that caused us stress.

The group described the usual issues that most people complain of, such as traffic, finances, dealing with difficult family members, and juggling the demands of work and home, all of which was standard and of no surprise. However, when my colleague and I shared that we often felt stress from the pressure we placed upon ourselves, Michael became excited and announced this would be our focus for the rest of the session.

He explained that all of the stressors of life we listed initially were external factors and somewhat out of our control but that the pressure we placed upon ourselves was an internal stress, and therefore deserved our attention and reflection.

Michael pulled no punches in his delivery and, over the course of the next thirty minutes, we learned what it meant to have a critical inner voice and the damaging impact that unchecked voice can have on our state of mind and well-being. We realised just how brutal the superego can be when it is constantly judging, shaming, or blaming, and how much suffering that inner dialogue can cause, leading us to believe that we are powerless and victims of circumstance.

Psychological concepts and insights that I had never before contemplated or heard were spoken about with passion, clarity and directness.

As the session unfolded, I became increasingly uneasy and emotional. I had the sense in the back of my mind that a Pandora's Box was opening up, which was both disorientating and surreal. Out of the box jumped the sudden realization that I was the one that had been causing myself pain through the negative narratives and judgements I had attached to my life. This profound insight was so intense and overwhelming to experience I felt like vomiting or running out of the room. No one else was to blame. Just me.

Hearing that truth and connecting to it in a way I never had before meant that I now had to take responsibility for myself and to stop playing the victim. There was a deep knowing that there would be no going back to who I had been before.

A moment of true awakening.

The sadness, grief and fear released that day continued long after the session ended. I cried tears for the time spent locked up in judgements and blame, tears for the lack of love and kindness I had shown to myself, tears for how disconnected I had been to my heart and truth, and tears for how scared I felt about not knowing who I would be without the old stories.

My heart ached.

From that point on, everything transformed.

Over the weeks, months and years that followed on from Michael's lessons, I pursued a path of healing, self-inquiry and personal development; I was motivated to let go of the toxic mindset and beliefs that had led to such a negative narrative in my mind and committed to making the pursuit of truth a guiding force.

Michael Bunting changed my life for the better. His lessons opened my eyes, set me on the path of awakening and taught me how to live deeply connected to my heart, for which I will be forever grateful.

"Only you can take responsibility for your happiness...but you can't do it alone. It's the great paradox of being human."

Simon Sinek

This is the amazing thing about the process. You ask someone to share gratitude for another, and this sparks love and gratitude to flow. This gratitude isn't just about you anymore; it gets multiplied. If you are present and understand what is happening, you'll see it is magical. Gratitude shows you care. Acknowledgment brings you into the moment and allows you to appreciate your life. It can turn famine into feast and darkness into light. It makes this moment enough.

SPREADING GRATITUDE

by Mollie McGlocklin

I recently hit my 2000th consecutive day of gratitude email messages to friends and family (aka 5.479 years of daily gratitude)! There is not a single habit that I've kept this consistently, and, in the process, this practice has taught me a lot.

Before starting this practice, I didn't hang out much in a state of gratitude regularly. For the most part, I hung out in a state of survival and suffering. Thanks to the repetition of this daily practice, mantra, or even prayer of gratitude, my mind is slowly but surely becoming more primed to seek out what's right versus what's wrong.

I've also discovered that you're never "done" with the practice of gratitude. It is a daily creation. Without working that muscle, our lizard brain will sail right back to everything that doesn't work. Bruce Lee once said, "I fear not the man who has practiced 10,000 kicks once, but I fear the man who has practiced one kick 10,000 times." I'm excited to see what life will look like after 10,000 days of gratitude.

Lastly, I've learned that sharing gratitude can be even more soul-filling than keeping it all to ourselves. The Gratitude Contagion Effect that happens when we don't keep our appreciation for our lives tucked away can be a win-win for both the listener and us.

That's why I'm grateful to be included in this book to help forward that goal of spreading gratitude as a collaborative and consistent part of life.

~

The more moments I collect, the more grateful I am. This isn't a gratitude jar where I'm writing down the things I'm grateful for. These are other people's instances of gratitude that are creating memories, moments, emotions, and reminders of the things I have to be grateful for in my life.

GATHERING GRATITUDE

"Alone we can do so little, together we can do so much."

Helen Keller

In the early stages of my gratitude-sharing idea, I was looking for new ways to get people to write letters. The idea was I would collect a week's worth of letters written to an individual, and that person would receive these gratitude letters every day for a week. It would be a surprise. The person would check their email or Facebook and see the letter was there to click on and read. This worked well. People who participated would then continue to share love for others. It was a circle of letter-writing love. We did a week for my grandma, one for my sister, one for each of my mom's best friends, one for my mom's cancer doctor, and so forth.

One of my sister's good friends, Amy, had been going to cancer treatments for months, and I wanted to do a campaign for her. In fact, I decided I would start two campaigns for her, one letter and one video. I traveled to her former workplace and gathered gratitude videos from her friends there. Also, my sister had a big gathering at her cabin and I collected more videos there. I had lots of letters come in from some of the people in the videos, too. In the end, I arranged two full weeks of letters and videos. I posted these love notes and videos so that she would get them when she was clear across the country, away from her family and friends, receiving treatments for her cancer.

GRATITUDE CUBED AND DEEP DIVES

"In real life, when you have an emotional experience, it's never just because of the thing that's been said. There's the backstory. It's like [Ernest] Hemingway's iceberg theory - the current emotional moment is the tip of the iceberg and all of the past is the seven-eighths of the iceberg that's underwater."

George Saunders

It's often said a good practice is to list three things we are grateful for every day. The idea is to take time, each day, to think about all the things and people we are grateful for in life.

The way to make things memorable and to create a more lasting impact is to list everything connected to the things we're grateful for as well. For instance, I am grateful for my coffee. I'm grateful for the water with which I make it, the beans, the machine in which I make it, the cup out of which I drink it, its warmth, and, after twenty minutes or so, the little perks the caffeine is going to give me.

Expressing gratitude in this way is much more powerful for the person, the person it's for, and the audience. It intensifies it, adding another dimension to the initial expression of gratitude.

The idea is taking the simple statement of what we are grateful for and expanding it. It will make our appreciation grow. This is wonderful to do when listing people we are grateful for in our life. For example, I am grateful for my dad. I'm not only grateful for my dad, but also for all the love, care, and support he has given me, for teaching me about love and dependability, for all the adventures and all the fun we've had together.

I am also grateful for water. I'm grateful I can drink it and use it in cooking and washing and cleaning. I'm grateful that it flows endlessly into my home twenty-four hours a day, seven days a week. I'm grateful that somewhere out there people are checking the water and filtering out elements that would be harmful to me. I'm grateful that I was born in this day and age so I don't have to travel great distances by foot to a lake or a stream or a well to collect it. I'm grateful that I have easy access to it at all times.

Let's take it a step further, I am grateful that I get to pay the water company every month for this amazing service that really is worth far more than its cost to me. I love this incredible life-sustaining substance that flows endlessly within steps of where I lay my head. I can think of all the people and all the time it took to lay the pipes and how the creation of new types of metal made it safer. Then there's the filter cover on the sink, the adjustable volume and pressure, and the adaptable temperature.

Naming what we're grateful for is the tip of the iceberg in relation to how amazing something or someone is and how much gratitude can be given.

FINDING GRATITUDE

"I THINK THEY LOOK COOL, DAD."

by Michael O'Brien

Michael O'Brien prevents bad moments from turning into a bad day and is the author of Shift: Creating Better Tomorrows; Winning at Work and in Life.

Years ago, when my youngest was eight years old, we were watching a movie together. As we watched, she stroked at my skin grafts because she wanted to see how they felt. After she finished, I asked her what she thought, and that's when she said that they looked cool. Then I started to cry.

Since my near-death cycling accident in 2001 that necessitated my skin grafts, I hated my scars. All I wanted to do was to cover them up because I thought everyone was staring at them. Many did, but I thought they looked at me with pity rather than strength.

But when she thought they were cool, something shifted within me. Kids can be brutally honest, and her perspective gave me a moment to see them differently. It made me wonder, could I see my scars as marks of resilience rather than imperfection?

So slowly, I started to see my scars through a lens of gratitude. They weren't ugly; they were merit badges that showed I survived something horrific. They were my indication that I was still alive.

A few years later, I discovered Kintsugi art, a Japanese art form called "The Golden Repair." It's a process where the artist takes broken pottery and mends it with gold, silver, or platinum fillet. It produces beautiful scar lines that transform the pottery from broken to better.

Today, I see my body, mind, and soul as Kintsugi art. I was once damaged and now better. My scars are something that I no longer hide from others; I show them with pride because our scars, wrinkles, blemishes, grey hairs and all tell our beautiful stories of resilience.

I'm grateful for that afternoon, eleven years ago, when my youngest helped me see my scars' beauty. Today, I know that I am, as we all are, beautiful.

～

"Some people could be given an entire field of roses and only see the thorns in it. Others could be given a single weed and only see the wildflower in it. Perception is a key component to gratitude. And gratitude is a key component to joy."

Amy Weatherly

THINKING

by Kevin Caldwell

Kevin Caldwell is a father and an author.

I've learned several impactful lessons in life, which has enhanced my thinking and added so much value. One of the most significant things I've learned is that limitation only exists in our mind. Truthfully, there are hindrances that will get us off task or may even challenge our progress. I have come to understand that those hindrances are called life. More importantly, my definition of those hindrances can lead to me achieving the outcome desired, or not. I'm grateful for my ability to be a critical thinker and ultimately know that if it is to be, the manifestation is on me!

THE POWER OF CONVERSATION

by Abbie Pierce

Abbie Pierce is a coach for creatives. She builds safe spaces for the awkward moments of learning, so that we can master the fear and practice the tenacity for sharing our creativity with the world.

As I sit alone at the computer every day and face a blank page, I often find myself asking, "What is this all for?"

Can I really have an impact and help people, while I reside in solitude and fumble my way through the fog?

As I retreat to the sofa for another episode of the Netflix series that is absorbing all my spare attention, my phone dings. I know that sound, it's a diary notification and probably nothing urgent. Besides, this episode is really gripping, and I don't want to miss what happens.

But as the curiosity and the habitual urge to check my phone becomes too great, I reach over to inspect the ding that has caused me to hit pause on the remote.

Shit! Shit! Shit! – I have a group discussion call in 30 mins. Damn, I forgot.

Then all sorts of excuses and stories start to bombard my mind and I try to slow things down enough so that I can extend my hand and grab one to hold on to. Those reasons usually include things like I won't be missed, it's not that important and I can always go next week.

And then another urge starts to take over. One that pulls at the things I value most like, trust, creativity, honesty and joy.

How can I live by my values when the fog is so thick, and I am all alone?

The pang of guilt begins to well because I know I am better than this and I have a moral duty to show up and contribute; it's important. So I peel myself off the sofa, fluff my hair and put on my Zoom top, before sitting down to the black screen and tap the power button.

The screen springs to life and I make the necessary clicks and taps to bring the browser into view. The Zoom link is before me and is begging to be activated, as I hesitate once more, still wondering if this was the right decision... to delay my Netflix daily dose in favour of an activity with no discernible direction and little known outcomes.

Just click it!

There we all are in our small thumbnail Brady Bunch style windows, all crammed into a screen, the playing field levelled and each with an open invitation to say something.

What is this really for? What can I say? What will they think? I might look foolish.

Then the anxiety and fear disappears because there is no room for that here. The space is filled by the conversation, and all I need to do is listen and see, give each person their moment of space and hold it for them, ask questions and stay curious. And then it's my turn, and they are generous and gracious in return.

That's the magic. The magical exchange of speech and hearing, as it takes a detour through the grey matter perfectly preserved in your head. The words spark thought, leading to consideration and finally insight or ideas. My worldview has changed, and now I have something to say.

The fog lifts. The blank page fills. I am not alone, even as I sit at my desk in solitude.

Endless gratitude for the power of conversation.

TRUST

by Bobsy Gaia

One of the most profound, long lasting lessons I have ever learnt came from my encounter with a street beggar in Hong Kong back in 1993. One early evening I was rushing to catch my ferry back to Lamma Island, an outlying Island here in Hong Kong, where I live. I only had ten minutes to make it to the gates. As I rushed along the Exchange Square footbridge, my eyes made contact with this street beggar, whom I had often spotted sitting quite serenely amongst people's busy feet in the midst of their oblivion to his presence. The serenity in his eyes made me stop in my rush, and I automatically proceeded to give him the only HK$10 in my pocket, and in my bank account for that matter. I was aware that I was giving away my last pennies and my only way to get back home, yet it strangely felt like the right thing to do. The ferry ride back in those days was HK$ 9.5. Without thinking twice, I smiled at him and continued on my way to Pier No 4. Upon arriving at the ferry gates, the fact that I had no money to get on board made me smile to myself in amusement at my predicament. Fortuitously, I spotted a friend boarding the ferry and asked him nicely if he would lend me HK$10 to get home. He did, and I got home safe and sound to my lovely farmhouse, which I was renting, in North Lamma. Even though I had no more money, I felt quite serene and liberated. A sense of freedom washed over me and I felt rather empowered, because there I was, penniless, not worried or anxious or too concerned about what came next. A sense of peace put me to bed that night. The next morning I woke up as usual and went to check on my letter box at the end of the charming path. Lo and behold there was an envelope with a cheque made out to me in the princely sum of HK$10,000. That bright sunny morning, overlooking the South China Sea, I learnt the power of trust.

JAMES'S LETTER

by Nicola Davies

Trust has always been a biggy for me, trust in romantic relationships, in work colleagues, in people in general, or in life itself. Even
when I would begin to feel that I could trust, just on that cusp of
believing and my shoulders relaxing, bang! There it was, sweet
deceit.

It was the hard way that I learned never to trust, because I would
always be proven wrong to the point I could say, "See? I told you!"

Little did I know I was setting myself up to be let down. My
walls had become so high that I had totally isolated myself. I
believed that I was happy that way and that it was far safer.

Then I met a lady who read and reviewed my book that was on
Amazon, and she said something positive that highlighted an aspect
I hadn't before considered, so I asked her to elaborate.

We chatted quite a bit and slowly became friends. Many a time I
would both knowingly and unknowingly test her trust, her every
word and action, and, over the course of a year, she never faltered,
not once. She said what she meant and meant what she said, and her
yes was yes, and her no, no.

I came to the conclusion that this world needs more people like
her: kind, compassionate, meek, and so very patient. I figured I
could never be like her. The way of this world as we know it doesn't
allow for such people, and I, a great sinner in my time, didn't have it
in me to be so genuinely calm hearted and giving. As for patience, I
had none, for anyone.

Initially, I felt an attraction to her but couldn't pinpoint what it
was exactly. It scrambled my mind that had been so absolute, so
definite that such people do not exist. Even when I told her of my
attraction, she still did not stumble but gave genuine upbuilding

words and comfort, and we sallied forth with our heads held high, she more eloquently than I.

She introduced me to a guy named James. He had written a letter which was published some time ago and, in it, had laid a solid foundation for the path that was awaiting me.

I drew close to him not really knowing what to expect and, gradually, over time, he too drew close to me, and my life began to change. My path began to straighten, life felt easier to endure, and I found more friends who share the same compassion.

Trust, as we know it, is a cruel and manipulative thing that changes people only adding to the ways of the world that we live in. We give our trust to people who lie, give mixed messages, back bite, are greedy, revolve around money, and ridicule. But there are a few out there who are the salt of the earth, demonstrate real truth, are honest from the core, and give out such deep genuine care. This world as we know it won't last much longer, but we do have just enough time to discover that truth, feel the difference as our paths straighten. And there isn't a single soul who isn't capable or worthy of such positivity.

So, go, find James, read his letter, and keep seeking the truth, true people, real people, and witness for yourself just how true his letter really is.

~

Gratitude is very much in the same realm as meditation. Gratitude brings us into the present moment and allows us to appreciate the things, people, opportunities, and privileges we have.

Let's take a moment, stop reading this book, and look up. What do we see? What is good? Most of us see a nice space that is ours or a space that is comfortable. We should be grateful for that space. We might feel cool air on our face or coolness in the room from the fan or air conditioner. We should be grateful for the fan or the air conditioner. Those of us who are safe and not in a war zone or running for our lives shouldn't be taking it for granted. We might have some sort of beverage that we are enjoying, a beverage that could be hot or cold. We should be grateful for the beverage and for this choice. We may be sitting on a piece of furniture. We should be grateful for that chair or sofa. Someone made that piece of furniture. We should be grateful for that person. We might be sitting on the floor. We should be grateful for a solid floor.

Now let's step a little further in. The place we are sitting may be uncomfortable. Just the fact that we can feel this discomfort in our body is something to be grateful for. The fact that we live in a day and age where we are educated enough to read and have access to books is something we might take for granted, but this has not been a reality for most people. In the past, even when there were books to read, very few knew how to read. There have been times in history when certain books were not allowed and even times when learning to read was nearly impossible. Reading is another freedom we should be grateful for.

I read all the time and this gratitude completely escapes me. Sitting to write about looking up from the screen, though, which is a thought experiment, has allowed me to appreciate this very thing I do multiple times a day, every day. I'm grateful that I can read, that I've been educated to do this, that I have the freedom to do this, that I have access to books, and that someone wrote the books I read. I'm thankful.

MY MAGICAL KEYCHAIN

by Ava Safran

Ava Safran is a copy editor and an English instructor. She is currently working on her first book, a creative nonfiction.

During the last two decades, I've been teaching ESL (English as a Second Language) part-time. Initially, I took the job to supplement my income and to have some kind of social life. Editing is quiet, and it can get lonely. I thought teaching would allow me to meet a few people, and I was right.

Teaching has been such a rewarding experience. I've met hundreds of wonderful people from around the globe over the years. They've taught me a lot about other cultures, and I have had the opportunity to help them learn to communicate in English.

On the last day of class, we always celebrate our time together with various dishes from different countries. Sometimes my students spoil me and express their thanks with little presents, flowers, cards, or simply cute notes.

A few years ago, a Japanese student gave me a keychain with a doll attached to it. At the moment I received the present, I thought it was just a cute keychain. When I got home, I looked at it more carefully and saw a label under the doll: Kimmidoll Collection Ayame

I got curious and went on their website. I found hundreds of dolls' pictures, each with a name and a description, all listed in alphabetical order. I found Ayame "Gratitude" easily. Its description read: "My spirit brings prosperity, happiness and fulfilment. You release my power by nurturing within yourself a spirit of appreciation. By valuing yourself, others and everything you have, you can enjoy a full and rewarding life."

I immediately fell in love with this tiny gratitude doll and decided not to use it as a keychain because I didn't want it to break or get chipped, so instead of carrying it around, I hung it on the wall right above my desk.

Every day, when I sit at my desk to edit, write, prepare lesson plans, or meet my students online, there she is, reminding me to nurture within myself a spirit of appreciation, and, every day, I feel filled with gratitude.

I look around and deeply appreciate every single thing I see, from the chair I'm sitting on to my laptop on my desk to my bookshelves which hold all my books. I'm thankful for the books I use daily, those I have so enjoyed reading, and those I have yet to read. I am thankful for the authors who wrote these books. I am grateful for my jobs that have allowed me to purchase these books.

I look at the window through which I see my beautiful roses out in the garden, the roses I care for every day. I see our lemon tree. I feel grateful for water and sunshine... and lemons.

Around me I see walls covered with framed photos of my family and friends, people who have given me so much love, people I'm so grateful to have in my life.

I feel the magic of gratitude every time I see Ayame. My beautiful Ayame doll makes me forget everything that hasn't gone right and focus on everything I have been blessed with so far. Whatever fairy dust she sprinkles fixes my perspective instantly. Any negative thought is suddenly replaced by positivity and hope and possibility.

I am infinitely grateful to my student who gave me Ayame, and I wish her the same magic she and the gratitude doll have brought into my life.

A CHOICE

by Danielle Moody

I am a full time mother, who in her previous life was an investment banker and recruiter. I made the choice to fully engage in raising our two sons and provide the sanctuary, comfort and support of a loving home. This, with my very supportive husband, has been our goal and we have achieved it while living over three countries. Being presented with the opportunity to manage this is something I am eternally grateful for. Preparation and planning in my early life, along with unwavering faith from my husband, has been the catalyst for our success. Now, with our eldest completing his final year of secondary abroad, I have had the opportunity to contemplate what we have managed and the outcome. I can reflect with enormous gratitude on having generous friends who have emotionally supported me, while I tried to parent two sons across two hemispheres. This was a struggle. I had a plan, but my sons had a very different one. I had the option of shutting down another individual's dream to stay true to my own desires, or enable them to explore their own possibilities. This was a defining moment where I could choose to be selfish or to grow and see what evolved. My perspective of life had to be completely altered, not in any small way, but entirely. When you alter your perception of a situation and your perspective of how it can unfold and make choices to achieve the perceived goal, everything is possible.

During this experience, we as a family had to make choices and change how we all perceived our relationships, how we all related to each other given our newfound distance, and how overtime this would shape our future selves. I struggled with this new family model as it wasn't in my plan. My perspective had been tipped on its axis and completely thrown off course. Thankfully, during this time, both sons were able to carve out new identities away from each other and respectively thrive. My perception of each boy evolved as well. I easily recognise them as two strong individuals who have very different qualities to take into the world.

The choice we reluctantly agreed to has been the right one. I can only now say that with unwavering gratitude as I see the results. Over the last few years, I have found gratitude to be the beacon I reach for during challenging times. When we reconfigure our focus, recalibrate our attitude and reflect on our result, we can live a happier, more peaceful and more composed life.

TURNING GUILT INTO GRATITUDE

by Isabella Williams

In my brief 22 years on earth, I've been extremely fortunate. I am the daughter of two incredibly driven and open-minded individuals who made the decision to experiment with living abroad from Australia for a few years. Twenty years later, they have still yet to return from an evidently never-ending adventure. I was three years old when we relocated to Singapore.

Singapore was special in that it facilitated a beautifully diverse childhood through exposure to new cultures, people, foods and experiences within a safe (though at times rigid) environment. Over the next nine years, our family of three grew to a family of six following the arrival of my two sisters and my brother. We then moved to Hong Kong, which slowly but surely blew my mind. A fast, crowded, edgy city filled to the brim and bursting at the seams with culture and innovation, Hong Kong moulded my adolescence in unexpectedly profound ways.

To have grown up within such an environment, yet to also know I was only there because of my parents, filled me with a sense of insecurity, because I knew I hadn't "earned" my place in this lifestyle. I came to feel increasingly guilty for my blessings, which only fuelled a growing anxiety based on the precariousness I perceived within my position. I began to wonder why I felt so guilty for being born into these circumstances, which ultimately I had no choice in.

Having moved to Melbourne three years ago to pursue a degree in Anthropology, Media and Communications, I've since been able to better contextualise myself in relation to the world around me. I've come to recognise guilt as a useless emotion in juxtaposition to gratitude, which can easily be converted into a positive driving force. Why feel guilty about something that no one has a say in?

Guilt for anything out of our control is a waste of both time and opportunity.

I've found it easy to spiral down one tangent of thought, particularly pessimistic ones, during times of uncertainty or stress. After slowly beginning to actively practice gratitude on a regular basis, I found the frequency with which I had previously tended to drift off on negative thought tangents significantly diminished. I think this can be accounted for by the ability of conscious gratitude to better put things into perspective and provide the motivation required to optimise good fortune.

Key to implementing a gratitude mindset is actively practicing it. One of my favourite, most rewarding aspects of practicing gratitude is expressing it to the people I admire. I've realised that oftentimes we forget to tell the people who need to hear it the most just how much we appreciate them. A most recent materialisation of this resulted in a spontaneous conversation with my housemate, who has been learning how to write and perform an Acknowledgement of Country.

Such a practice is performed with intent to show respect to the traditional owners of Australian land, of which sovereignty has never been ceded by First Nations people. To me, Acknowledgements of Country are, in part, a manifestation of gratitude in that they strive to ground listeners by reminding them of the origins of Australia, which are deeply rooted in a history of indigenous oppression and exclusion that non-indigenous Australians continue to benefit from today.

This example of active gratitude demonstrates how guilt can be transformed into a positive driving force through recognition, humility and respect. Gratitude has and will no doubt continue to inform my sense of self in many ways, not only as a means of expressing appreciation for the opportunities my blessings have afforded me, but also by propelling me into a future riddled with optimistic possibility.

THANK GOD FOR MY WEAKNESSES

by Sha Nacino

Sha Nacino is the author of 14 books, a keynote speaker on gratitude &
creativity, and the founder of the World Gratitude Summit. In 2019, she
was awarded as the Female Entrepreneur of the Year by the United
Nations Global Entrepreneur Council.

I remember the "me" before.

I was too shy, too introverted.

I've always been shy ever since I was young.

When I was in grade school and you would ask my teachers, aunts, uncles, cousins, and relatives to describe me using one word, that word would be "shy."

I've been so shy for as long as I can remember.

In college, I wouldn't dare raise my hand during recitation because I was so scared to be noticed.

When I started working for a bank, I hardly talked to my office-mates. If I had to talk to them, I had to practice what I had to share.

My shyness was a burden for me; it was my greatest weakness! I was so shy that I was shy, and I felt so uncomfortable being shy.

Even when I became an author, I was still too shy.

When people approached me or talked to me, I wanted to hide.

After I wrote my first book and my first few books, so many people wanted to treat me to lunch or dinner or snacks.

Their reason? They wanted me to teach them how to write a book.

I felt so uncomfortable with their invitations.

And I complained to God,

"God, why am I so painfully shy?

Why am I so introverted?

Why is it so hard for me to communicate with people?"

I would even catch myself crying because I couldn't understand why I had to be too shy and introverted.

But God also placed in my heart the desire to serve sincerely.

So I thought of a way to teach these people how to write a book and, at the same time, respect my being shy and introverted.

I studied the world of internet. I studied how to create an online course, and I put up an online course on book writing.

Shy No More

Slowly, as I focused more on serving other people through doing what I love to do, I became less shy and less introverted.

Today, I feel so comfortable talking to people from all walks of life: janitors, drivers, cleaners, CEOs, entrepreneurs, helpers, global speakers, celebrities, and so on.

I've also interviewed some of the people I look up to like Jack Canfield, Dr. John Demartini, Hal Elrod, Andrew Matthews, Dr. Ivan Misner, to name a few.

To date, we have now launched several online courses and online summits like the HR Summit Global, World Gratitude Summit, Global Authors Summit, Write a Book Summit, Overseas Filipinos Summit, etc.

Then the Covid-19 global pandemic happened.

Offices closed.

Travels stopped.

Everything closed.

Even the events in the Philippines and abroad where I was supposed to speak on were cancelled as well.

The Gifts Behind my Weaknesses

And then I realized...

My weaknesses, my shyness and my being introverted, were GIFTS!

In the midst of the pandemic, my team and I are able to reach and serve thousands of people from all over the globe (in the comforts of our own homes) through our online courses and online summits!

If I hadn't been so painfully shy and introverted, I wouldn't have gone online as early as 2011!

If it hadn't been for my weaknesses, I wouldn't have my created online course which led me to create more online courses and eventually online summits!

My weaknesses prepared me and my business to thrive during this pandemic!

Our online summit, the HR Summit Global, which took place in April 2020, had over 10,000+ participants from 32 countries globally!

Our World Gratitude Summit that took place in August 2020 had over 15,000+ participants from 49 countries globally!

Your Weaknesses are Blessings in Disguise

What are your weaknesses?

Not outgoing enough? Too sensitive? Too emotional? A cry baby?

Too shy? Too loud? Too introverted? Too extroverted?

Whatever it is you are complaining about, be kind to yourself.

Then look at your complaints through the lens of Gratitude and Creativity.

Gratitude: What's good about this situation? What can I learn from this?

Creativity: How can I turn this complaint into an opportunity?

As you keep asking yourself these questions, you will realize that your weaknesses are not really weaknesses at all. Your weaknesses are beautiful blessings you have yet to unwrap.

GRACIAS...

by Viko

Gracias es una de las palabras que más utilizo a diario, me hace ser más consciente que nos debemos a las otras personas, significa que entiendes que eres parte de un todo y que, reconociéndote, desarrollándote y creciendo como individuo, es como más puedes aportar a construir una mejor coexistencia en el mundo. El individualismo no es sinónimo de egoísmo porque al final ese desarrollo que logras como ser humano en parte se lo debes a tantas personas, a esos momentos que vives y más aún cuando decides como vivirlos, como asumirlos, cuando decides a qué te aferras, en qué creer y en que no y eso va forjando tu carácter, es como si cada una de esas experiencias fuera una piedra, una piedra que te puede hacer tropezar pero también te puede ayudar a construir un camino.

En mi vida he tenido la gran fortuna y bendición de formar parte de una gran familia y contar con grandes amigos que siempre han sido mi sostén, en ellos veo todo lo que quiero en mi vida, ellos son el borde, son la guía de ese camino que sigo construyendo y no tendré nunca como agradecer lo suficiente por eso.

Ya con el tiempo aprendes cómo las personas actúan desde sus propias vivencias, sus propias alegrías y sus propios miedos, aprendes tanto de lo malo que te muestra lo que no quieres ser, como de lo bueno que quieres replicar y hace mucho decidí ver todas esas vivencias como lecciones, unas me gustaron otras no, unas me rompieron el alma, otras no, y después de todo esto sólo ves como de a poco te vas reconstruyendo, de a poco vas moldeando tu mejor versión, vas decantando o la vida lo hace, no lo sé, te hace ver lo esencial por encima de la necesidad y el deseo, y pueda que eso signifique menos cosas, menos personas, pero también menos carga y eso te da más tranquilidad, plenitud, es cuando por fin se apaga el ruido ensordecedor del mundo y te puedes escuchar, y te puedes reconocer entre tantas figuras, es ahí cuando te descubres a ti mismo.

Sé que no todo puede ser felicidad y está bien, habrá momentos difíciles y eso también está bien, porque esa dualidad es la que te mantiene en equilibrio, me quedo con la certeza de la incertidumbre, me quedo con saber vivir mejor un día a la vez y agradeciendo por ello...

Thank you...

Thank you is a word that I say a lot on a daily basis. It makes me more aware that we need one another. It means that you understand that you are part of a whole and that by recognizing yourself, developing yourself, and growing as an individual, you can contribute the most to building a better coexistence in the world.

Individualism is not synonymous with selfishness because in the end that development you achieve as a human being is partly due to so many other people. It's due to those moments you live and even more so when you decide how to live them and how to assume them, when you decide what you cling to, in what to believe, and what not to believe. These things that are forging your character, it is as if each of those experiences were a stone, a stone that can make you stumble but can also help you build a path. In my life I have had the great fortune and blessing of being part of a great family and having great friends who have always been my support; in them I see everything I want in my life. They are the edge, they are my guides on the path that I continue to build and I can never thank them enough for that.

Over time you learn how people act from their own experiences, their own joys, and their own fears. You learn how you don't want to be and the good you want to replicate. I decided long ago to see all those experiences as lessons, some I liked, others I did not, some broke my soul, others did not. After all this you only see how little by little you are rebuilding, little by little you are shaping the best version of yourself, you choose or life does. I don't know if it makes you see what's essential above need and desire, and that may mean fewer things, fewer people, but also less burden and that will give you more peace of mind, fullness; that's when all becomes quiet, the deafening noise of the world, and you can hear yourself, and you can recognize yourself among so many figures; that's when you discover yourself. I know that not everything can be happiness and it is fine; there will be difficult moments, and that is also good because that duality is what keeps you in balance. I am left with the certainty of uncertainty; I am left with knowing how to live better one day at a time. I am grateful for this.

WASTING A GIFT

The next time you are rushing around from one place to the next, remember this quote I collected from an episode of GratitudeSpace Radio. If we can't stop to appreciate the good in our life, is it really good? We can't stop and appreciate every little thing all day long. It would be ideal, but it is not realistic. We can easily start by putting a note next to our alarm or a calendar reminder on our phone that says *bed*.

Those of us who have a bed should appreciate our bed. We have a place to sleep at night, possibly our own pillow, clean blankets, and the ability to clean them. Millions of people go to sleep every night and don't have a bed. Many don't have a home... or even a shelter.

Many may feel entitled and say they worked hard to own a bed. Just because we own something doesn't mean we can't appreciate it and be grateful for it.

LITTLE THINGS

by Elizabeth Holland

Elizabeth Holland is an author of romance novels and a mental health blogger. Her first novella focused on mental health (with a side of romance). The Balance Between Life and Death is a reminder that you never know what someone else is going through.

I think it's safe to say that at some point during our lives we've all been guilty of taking something or someone for granted. It's not always something we consciously do; life just gets in the way.

Over the last few years, my struggles with my mental health (emetophobia, depression and anxiety) have meant that I've learned to take a step back and appreciate the smaller things in life. It's not been easy but it has been necessary. I believe that happiness lies within gratitude and therefore being grateful for the small things is essential for daily happiness.

You might be reading this thinking, 'what little things are there to be grateful for?' Well, let me tell you what I'm grateful for today that I may have once taken for granted.

A fancy coffee from a coffee shop - During my time at university I was guilty of having multiple cups of these a day (goodbye student loan). These days, a coffee out is a rare treat and I enjoy savouring every moment. From the taste to the joy of drinking something that I haven't made - there are lots of reasons to be grateful for a simple cup of coffee.

Seeing family and friends - 2020 has been the year that I've realised just how grateful I am for my family and friends. Before the pandemic I would see my family a few times a week and they would support me with my mental health struggles. During lockdown in the UK I was unable to see them for weeks on end. I've promised myself to never take them or their support for granted again.

Music - I've definitely taken music for granted in the past. Recently I've realised just how important it is and how grateful I am. The right song can really improve your mood and your day.

The sun shining - The weather has a huge influence on my mood and so when the sun's out I automatically feel a little happier. I try to be grateful for these sunny days and make the effort to go outside, even if it's only for a few minutes.

Exercise - Recently exercise is something that I've become incredibly grateful for. It's also something that I've taken for granted in the past. However, over the last few months I've discovered what a positive impact it can have on my mood.

...

Finding gratitude in the little things has really helped me cope with my anxiety and depression. If I look for the good in each thing I do, it helps to put a smile on my face, even if it's just for a few minutes each day. Learning to slow down enough to stop taking things for granted is a skill and one that I think we could all benefit from learning.

Take the time to slow down and be grateful for the things that you once took for granted.

GRATITUDE SWINGS BIG DOORS

If we think of our life as an ever swinging or revolving door, because of time, we are always walking through it. Sometimes it opens a little and we squeeze through, and other times it opens wide and we stroll right through. It's either one or the other; it's either this or that, squeeze or stroll. The truth is it's either gifts or lessons. It's that simple; let's not make it any more difficult. It's just gifts or lessons.

My friend Rajesh Setty was the first person to share this idea with me in his Mindvalley Talk and also in his book, *Gratitude: Grow & Change Your World One Thank You at a Time.*

This idea was also reinforced By Shawn Stevenson, the host of The Model Health Show when he came on GratitudeSpace Radio. His definition of gratitude was, "I'm always looking for the gift in things, and when things are challenging, I am tuning back into the things I have to be grateful for right now, through this challenge, and that is what being grateful means to me."

It's easy to be grateful for a gift. Someone gives us a gift or buys us lunch. We would naturally say *thank you* and express our appreciation for the gift. That's what I call *easy gratitude.*

A more complex form of gratitude is being thankful for life's lessons. Now with the small hinge swinging just enough to let us squeeze through, we can say, "I know this is hard right now, and what is happening might be awful, but I will find a life lesson in all of this. I am being taught something, and for that I am grateful."

If we don't prime our thinking, we are unconsciously deciding not to learn and making things worse not only for us but for everyone around us. That would be closed-door, ungrateful thinking.

With open-minded, expanded thinking, what we are really doing is giving a gift to our constantly improving self. It's a lesson we learn that will serve us.

Gratitude is the gift that keeps on giving. Gratitude guides both what we see and what we don't, what we believe we can and can't do. Gratitude is an abundance mindset.

Gratitude can help us realize that material things won't bring us happiness. Living in gratitude allows us to know that we are enough, instead of the usual model of I will be enough when X happens, or I will be happy when…

We have a choice to be either grateful or ungrateful. Gratitude is the hinge that swings big doors. We can take control, be a hero, be grateful, and see abundance.

ASHES

by Diane Riley

Diane Riley is a former journalist, proofreader, and copy editor. Her favorite thing in the whole wide world is reading; researching comes in at a close second. She is currently writing her first novel.

Today I showed my husband, Steve, where I want my ashes tossed. The location is my favorite spot in the world—really, in the whole wide world: Goose Rocks Beach in Maine.

Almost 30 years ago, when I was a single mom, I decided to take my daughter on vacation. It would be a time of relaxation, a time of fun, a time where she could bring a friend, leaving a bit of emotional space between a mother and a tween. A coworker suggested a fishing village called Cape Porpoise, which is part of Kennebunkport. He showed me photos of the small, red cottage he and his wife rented each summer for a week. He warned me that Cape Porpoise was a fishing village, quiet, out of the way, no thrills or chills. Just what I wanted.

That led to a few years of annual vacations, renting from a wonderful woman named Mrs. Craig. Her husband had been captain of a fishing vessel. She had been born and raised in Cape Porpoise and had so much to share with her stories and photos. The small red cottage was nothing much: twin beds, a couch, a very small kitchen, a very small porch. It was nestled under a grove of trees that helped keep it cool in the summer. Unfortunately, mosquitoes liked the area too, but that didn't matter. We were on vacation.

The local beach is Goose Rocks. We went down there just about every day to play in the sand and the waves. The sand is very fine and white; the waves are very small because of the break stones on both sides. Two or three islands can be reached at low tide.

One day when I was walking along the beach at low tide, just when the ocean was starting its return to higher ground, I came across a spot that to me seemed almost sacred (and still does). If you were to face the ocean while standing on Goose Rocks Beach, you would turn and walk left until you came to a creek/river that empties into the ocean. At low tide, a narrow peninsula is revealed, with the river water on the left and the ocean in front and to the right.

I walked to the end point and was mesmerized. The waves were coming from the right and the left, joining at the end of the point. The sound of the breaking waves was musical. The designs on the sands like fine works of art. Warm inland water meshed with cooler ocean water, clear water with salt. The inland water pushed out as the ocean water pushed in, creating a tension that was oh so gentle. I stood as long as I could to watch, listen, sigh, pray, wonder. As the tide continued to come in, the water pushed me back. Every year we go to the ocean I visit that spot just at the right time: when the tide starts coming back in.

Many years after first discovering that spot, I was diagnosed with ovarian cancer, stage 3c. Funny things go through your mind when diagnosed with something that will eventually kill you. How long? Do I make a bucket list? Do I fight or give in? What about death? Where do I want my ashes to go? Amid the eddies of emotions and planning, I remembered Goose Rock Beach. During that time of turbulence, I was grateful for a small mercy: I knew where my ashes would go.

Today I was able to show the space to Steve. I had described the location a bit, but I had to show him, to make sure he got it right. He too saw the beauty of the yin and yang. He pointed out the island in front, the rocky beach on the right, the fordable river of inland water, the ocean forests.

Even on a gray early evening, leaning toward rain, the spot was perfect—sacred. We left in peace.

ON A MISSION

I went on a mission trip to Jamaica with a youth group the summer after my freshman year of high school. I have three random memories from that trip.

The first is the bus trip we took up into the mountains after we arrived in Jamaica. This was a long ride, five to six hours long. The funny thing about this bus ride to the mountains was that the bus driver stopped to smoke pot at least two times during this long drive. I saw this long wall built of rocks and my kid brain thought slaves must have built it. The countryside going into the mountains was beautiful. It was a completely different world up there, away from the city, its loud noises, crowd of people, tourists.

The second is the incredibly cold showers. We were all staying in a dorm with bunk beds. All the water we used came from rainwater. One of the leaders said that this was like a military shower: fast, get wet, soap up, rinse. Going to the bathroom had its own rules, too: if it's yellow, let it mellow; if it's brown, flush it down. One of the guys would pee a very long time every morning. Most of us would be awake when he'd go and time him on our watches. I believe one morning he peed for a minute and forty seconds. We were all very impressed, so much so that twenty-five years later, I still remember it.

The third is that we had to haul rocks and concrete up this hill that had to be over fifty yards. We were there to build a house, but it was like a vacation for us Louisville folks traveling to a tropical island for two weeks to have fun, gain new experiences, and build a house in the mountains. We only helped build the foundation during our trip. The next group would continue with the building. The man we were building the house for was a very kind and hard-working Jamaican. He had a wife and a daughter. He worked with us every day. One day, he invited us all to his little home. We met his wife and daughter. His wife cooked for all of us. I was a picky eater at the time and didn't really like the food. But I knew that this was a big thing for her to cook for us. These were poor people, and making this lunch was her way of saying thanks, so I ate it all. I felt they really appreciated me for this work I'd done. This was a powerful demonstration of gratitude that I experienced.

PERSEVERANCE PAYS

by Gail Boenning

Gail is a longtime wife, mother, animal aficionado, and wanderer who devotes her life to curiosity, learning, and connecting. Like a river, she's forever flowing and changing.

The greatest gift lies in seeing who they are instead of who you want them to be.

At 8:47 p.m. I received a text message from my son. There were no words—only a simple photo of his hand holding a folded bundle of twenty dollar bills. Further explanation was not necessary. The picture was truly worth a thousand or more words and one hundred and eighty bucks.

The photo told the story of a lifetime of passion and grit...a case study of how to live your dreams, starring a young man, age 15.

Want to hear??? Huh? Huh? Want to? Want to?

Cuz I really want to share.

N first went fishing somewhere between the age of two and three. His dad took him over to the pond at a local park with a Styrofoam container of earthworms and a purple 'Lil Rhino fishing pole.

The child was hooked.

There are twelve years of fishing stories between that first fishing trip and the cash winnings I saw pictured in his text—maybe a story for each one of those one hundred and eighty dollars. Stories of kayaks, Christmas gifts, boat surprises, YouTube channels, plastic lures made on our gas grill and taxidermy. There just might be enough stories to fill an entire book. I might write that book someday, but for today, I'll summarize.

The 18-inch, largemouth bass was a second place finisher, earning my kid his first tournament win. After twenty plus outings at fifteen dollars a try, sweet success finally called. He's on the board. He told me it was the best day of his entire year, which is saying something as the winning fish was caught on September 14th.

The thing is, neither his father nor I at his birth thought, Wouldn't it be nice if our son was obsessed with fishing? It would be so lovely if we could talk about fish, lures, lakes, rivers, rods, boats, homework (just kidding), tournaments and ALL things fishing, non-stop, ad nauseam.

You see, his dad might have preferred a speed skating, NFL tight end with an engineering degree.

I would have basked in the presence of a kind, outgoing volunteering sort, always offering to lend a hand, while maintaining stellar grades and a clean room.

Neither of our "visions" are fully coming to pass. He is a good student, a kind of kind person for a teenage boy, and he does speed skate and play football on an average level.

But, he is who HE is and we would not want it any other way.

I am glad that we have both been able to see into his soul. I am glad that our grumbling has not deterred him from his love and passion. I am glad we bought a boat and that his dad turns his work life on end to make it home in time for the Wednesday tournaments.

I hope someday he will make a living and a life doing what he loves.

And I hope, if he has children one day, he will give them the gift of recognizing who they are.

GRATITUDE IS CONTAGIOUS

"Recognizing the gift of 'being'."

Prince Ea (GratitudeSpace Interview 2016 - when asked what gratitude meant to him)

Gratitude breeds gratitude. It's contagious.

My gratitude for my mother led me to all the corners of this country seeking out others' gratitude in the hope that this gift would be seen. It's right in front of us. Many of our experiences exist because of countless others, and with a little thought and mindfulness, we can see each connection and appreciate it.

BUTTERFLY

by Girma Bishaw

Girma Bishaw is the director and founder of Gratitude Initiative.

Gratitude helps us see a butterfly in a caterpillar.

"Walking in the nearby forest with Granddad was the most joyous and educational time of my childhood," Ola said to me, sinking in deep thought. "My Granddad used every conversation to educate me about life and living well. He used to make me laugh a lot; he was so funny. I am forever grateful for the opportunity of being with him for the first 12 years of my life.

"I remember one day, we were doing our usual daily walk in the nearby forest, slowly talking, Granddad speaking, me asking questions. We made it to the middle of the forest, where frequent camping and hiking made this particular area exposed. As we stood for a while, debating what had caused this region of the woods to be so popular, a caterpillar crept out from the crumpled grass. Without a moment's hesitation, I raised my foot to crush it. Understanding what I was about to do, Granddad grabbed my foot and stopped me. I looked at Granddad, perplexed; 'But it's so ugly' I said. That day Grandpa taught me a lesson that formed a lasting perspective of the way I view the world.

"Grandpa didn't say much until we came out of the forest. Once we were out of the field, beautiful butterflies filled the air, flying around from one wildflower to the other. I chased after them, laughing and giggling. Granddad watched me for a minute, and then he called me and asked why I was running after the butterflies. I said, 'Look Grandpa they are so beautiful.' He said, 'Do you know that these butterflies were like that caterpillar which you were about to kill a while ago?' I waited, expecting the punchline; but there was none. I thought he was joking but soon understood that he was serious. 'How on earth is that even possible?' I asked. He said, 'Through time,' and explained to me in the simplest way possible how the transformation occurs. I was quiet for a little while and felt sad at the thought of killing a butterfly.

"My Granddad then said, 'You see, in life, time changes everything. You have to understand that in every ugly situation, there is a potential for beauty. You have to be patient. People who disagree with you, people who don't like you, people who are different from you, from where you are standing, they may look bad. Still, if you handle them correctly, they all contribute to your progress. In every bad situation, in the people you may dislike, there is a potential for beauty, given time, patience, and the right environment. Don't rush to kill, to judge, to hate but be grateful that in all things there is a potential for beauty.'

"Years later, I was sitting at reception, waiting to be called for a job interview. Several people turned up for the same interview. I was sitting near the receptionist. I could tell that she was from a tribe which was in fierce animosity with my own. Of course, she could also tell which tribe I was from. I could sense her initial hostility towards me. I was sure she loathed the idea of me working with her in the same company. If it were up to her, I would have been out of the door with no doubt. On occasion, I caught her glaring at me and mumbling curse words under her breath.

"However, I did not return her bitterness, and I wasn't full of hate towards her or her tribe. My family taught me to treat individuals not by their birthplace but by their character. My Granddad used to say, 'Be grateful that there are people where you are. What would life look like, if it was just you, living on this planet?'

"As the number of interviewees decreased, leaving the premises after their interview, I plucked up the courage to go and speak to the receptionist. I asked, 'Are you from ---?' mentioning her town's name. With a face that expressed mixed emotions: anger, hatred and surprise, 'Yes,' she replied bluntly, and continued what she was doing.

"Persistent, I went on, 'Two years ago, I was driving through your town, and there was terrible weather. I ended up moving out of the road into a ditch. It was evening, getting dark and raining heavily, so I ended up sleeping in my car overnight. In the morning, someone saw my car and came with some more people and volunteered to help me to push the car out of the ditch. Afterwards, they insisted that I should get warm and eat breakfast before I left. I submitted to their insistence. They fed me the most delicious breakfast (their traditional food), and later that day, I continued my journey. I remain grateful for their kindness. I don't remember experiencing such goodwill ever since, even from my own tribe.'

"Her composure totally changed. She asked me a few questions, smiling this time, like where I came from or whether I knew the weather forecast. Then I was asked to go to the interview room. It happened that I managed to get the job and started to work with my new receptionist friend soon after. It was later on, after a few months or so, that she told me she had plans to minimise my chance of getting the job. She said, 'Do you remember how you were given a form to fill when you come in for the interview?' I nodded. She said, 'I was about to go to the interviewer and tell him that you were struggling to fill the form and was asking for help from people beside you and that he shouldn't waste time on you.' She smiled guiltily at me, expecting my anger, but I laughed at her quick-witted thinking and thought nothing of it. She then told me what my gratitude story had done to her.

"'When you told me about your experience with my tribe, and how grateful you are for the kindness shown to you, I remembered what my mother said to me about a disabled man from your tribe who saved her brother from committing suicide. Her brother was a cattle merchant and one Saturday he went to the market to sell his cattle. On the way back from the market, he was robbed, and all his money was taken. That particular year hadn't been a good year for him. He had experienced a drastic loss in his property investments and was now in debt. So he decided to end it all. He went to a quiet area on the outskirts of the town, found a tree, and prepared to hang himself. There was a disabled middle-aged man from your tribe who lived in the area. He used to enjoy going out in the evenings with his son pushing him on his wheelchair. As he approached, he saw my uncle and realised what he was about to do. So he hurried his son towards my uncle as quickly as he could.

"'When he got to my uncle, he threw himself around his leg and begged him to listen to him. Eventually, my uncle was touched and, convinced by his persuasion, decided not to end his life. Through time and hearing negative stories about your tribe, I completely forgot the good my family experienced from your tribe. That day, your gratitude reminded me I also have something to be grateful about.' When she finished her story, I said, 'You see, gratitude begets gratitude.' And she added 'Gratitude also builds bridges and highlights the good.' I concluded, remembering what my granddad taught me, that gratitude also helps you see a butterfly in a caterpillar. She laughed and said, 'Are you supposed to be the caterpillar?'"

～

The struggle is real but so is our gratitude. Unfortunately, our minds have a negative bias. Ninety-nine people can compliment us, but if one person says something negative, we focus on that one negative thing and give it so much power that it makes us forget to be grateful. Let's live each day with a grateful heart. Let's take the time to say thank you. Let's look people in the eyes and appreciate however they are helping us. It doesn't matter if it's their job; they are people that we should be grateful for. So many people help us out daily. Let's walk out with the mindset that we are going to truly thank one person every day. Let's express why we are grateful and why it matters to us. Let's share our gratitude, and let it be a reflection to others to see their gratitude.

GRATITUDE IN TIMES OF
UNCERTAINTY

GRATITUDE & HOPE

by Noosha Ravaghi

Noosha Ravaghi is an author and a copy editor.

I was at the wrong place at the wrong time and witnessed something I shouldn't have, so I had to be publicly discredited. Consequently, my home, my cash, and my reputation were all taken away from me. My loyal companions were at risk, so they had to go to safety, far away. My car was broken into, and whatever I had left was stolen.

My most basic necessities were all gone. No shelter, no money, no real food, and no sleep. My insomnia prevented me from concentrating on anything. Homeless and deprived of any sense of safety and security, I was on autopilot and somehow managed to keep myself alive. All I had left was my integrity and my hope to get back what mattered to me most at the time: my three beloved dogs.

The day I rescued those dogs, I'd made a promise to them. I'd told them I would take care of them as long as I was alive. Well... I was still alive, and all I wanted was to be reunited with them and have a shelter for all four of us to be together.

For seventy-three days, the number of days I was homeless, I listed everything I still had. I had a car: I could sit and sleep in it; it could take me to visit my dogs and to the part-time jobs I had left. I had a credit card: It allowed me to buy gas for the car and enough food for me to stay alive. I had a membership to the 24-hour gym: I could use the bathroom and shower, day or night. I had clothes to wear: I could keep warm. I had my dogs' love: They were waiting for me to get things straightened out.

I had to remind myself several times a day that I still had these things, that I hadn't lost everything, that I was still alive. Being grateful gave me hope. Being grateful and having hope allowed me to stay on autopilot as long as it was necessary to get my life back little by little, starting with a temporary shelter, then the dogs, then work, then money.

When I had enough money, I was able to move, so I got myself and my dogs to safety, to a secure and somewhat permanent shelter, where I eventually started to get my ability to sleep back, and with that my health gradually came back, and so on.

It was my constant appreciation for the little I had left that reminded me there was still hope. Without that gratitude, I wouldn't be here today.

~

What about when we are struggling or when we experience a loss? We may feel there isn't much to be grateful for, but especially in those moments, gratitude can help. We can focus on the positive side of things by being grateful, or, as Lewis Howes said, by "being appreciative of what you DO have in your life instead of focusing on what you DON'T have." *(GratitudeSpace 2016 - when asked what gratitude meant to him)*

PERSPECTIVE

Perspective is everything. Right now we, all human beings, are experiencing a devastating pandemic. We are losing our acquaintances, neighbors, friends, and family members. It's terrible, and it seems like there isn't much to be grateful for. What we don't realize, though, is how the current crisis we are facing could be much, much, worse.

We could be living with no running water and not be able to bathe, shower, go to the bathroom, wash dishes... We could be without any drinking water, meaning no coffee, no tea... We could be left without electricity, meaning no lights, no power for appliances to prepare food, no refrigeration, no television, no computers for work or play, no video games, no movies, no cellphones, no internet. We could be without emergency service providers, meaning no fire department or doctors or nurses or police...

Thankfully, all of these are available. For this, we can be grateful. Things are not perfect, and they seem like the worst disaster on the surface, but when we stop and reflect, we realize we still have a lot to appreciate. Of course, it's important to follow all of the suggested guidelines and precautions, such as keeping a safe distance, wearing a mask, and staying at home as much as possible, but it's also important to be grateful for all we do have.

Instead of looking at these as punishment, we can look at them as opportunities to read that book we've been meaning to read, call that person we've been meaning to call, start that home project we've been putting off, or just relax, take a deep breath, and enjoy this forced pause.

This is a real crisis, and it needs to be taken seriously, but we shouldn't let it rob us of our joy, peace, and love. That stuff is ours, and when we worry about the things we can't control, we don't fix anything; we just let that worry take our mind away from all the good stuff that's going on in our life, and we lose control, and then panic sets in, and we suffer needlessly.

Of course, some of us have been personally, significantly, and adversely affected, and some of us have lost a loved one. For those of us affected in this way, these are sad times, but even in such difficult times, we still have a lot to be grateful for, and we should try to focus on the good and express our gratitude for what we have. If nothing else, it will help us through our difficult time. Gratitude is a coping tool we can use at any time to go deep inside to calm our mind and put things in their proper perspective.

DAD

by Adrienne Brown

The pandemic of 2020 sent a pulse that shocked the world. Businesses closed. Schools closed. People were confined to their homes. The virus was spreading across the globe and taking lives along the way. Eventually, the virus would come touch our family.

Dad,

COVID-19 took you away from our small family unexpectedly. We simply were not prepared to lose the quiet yet strong man who was the rock of our family. Our family of four that operated as a unit now has to recalibrate and learn how to live in a world without you.

Dad, you are the first person I ever truly mourned. Yes, I have had family members pass away, but I didn't know them the way I know you.

You were the first man I knew. I saw you as a hard worker, supporter and provider.

But I also saw you as a quiet man who didn't say much. Because of this (and because I am equally quiet), I was not able to connect with you.

When I was young, I was easily offended. One time, when I was in high school, I showed you a Social Studies test with a grade of a B. As a backstory, Social Studies was my worst subject. I was excited to get a B! When I showed you the paper, you looked it over and handed it back to me and said, "Why didn't you get an A"? I was crushed. I don't think I showed you another test grade from that point forward.

As I grew older, I realized that was your way of pushing me to do better.

Although you may not have said much, you were always available. When I needed to learn how to drive, you were my instructor. When I was working nights, you picked me up at the train stations. I realize that was how you showed how much you cared.

I think back to the time I had to get my wisdom teeth extracted as a teenager. It was my first time getting that type of procedure. You escorted me to the dentist. You sat in a chair next to me. You held my hand as the dentist administered the anesthesia. I closed my eyes hoping it would ease the pain (it didn't). When I turned to look at you, your eyes were closed tighter than mine! But you held my hand through the entire procedure.

You were also there during my recent battle. When I was diagnosed with breast cancer, you were there every step of the way.

During this journey, I saw how much we had both matured from the experience at the dentist almost forty years ago. You asked questions. You researched information. You talked to neighbors to understand what I was about to go through. If my husband couldn't come to a treatment, you were always available. You escorted me to every one of my radiation treatments. The last picture you and I took together was when I rang the bell at my final radiation treatment. You were the silent encouragement I needed.

To me, your favorite word was "ironic." You could find the irony in just about anything! There are three ironic events I took away from your untimely passing:

1. It is ironic you passed away in a hospital: You hated hospitals! You may have accompanied Mom, my brother, or myself to the hospital, but your facial expressions clearly showed you did not want to be there.

In March of 2020, you came down with something you could not shake. The doctor said it was strep throat, but you still wouldn't recover. When you walked into the hospital, I did not think that would be the last time I would see you.

2. You loved being around people, but you were alone in the hospital. You may not have said much, but you enjoyed the company of others. You attended all of the family reunions. You were physically active. You loved being a baseball coach and umpire. You would umpire softball games in the hottest and coldest weather. You loved people calling you for advice. You had standing telephone calls with family members. You were the designated driver on the family road trips to area casinos. You did all of this with your signature smile.

COVID-19 restrictions prevented us from visiting you. We called to talk to you everyday until you were placed on the ventilator. Afterwards, we had to rely on doctors to provide updates. We couldn't see you, so the entire family got together on a conference call and prayed for you with our pastor. Mom, my husband and I drove to the hospital and got as close as we could and prayed: my brother was on the phone listening and praying.

3. I couldn't hold your hand. On April 17, 2020, our family received the dreaded call: the hospital staff was going to prepare for my dad's transition. The hospital arranged for a FaceTime connection, so my Mom, my brother and I could "see" you. When I saw your face appear on the monitor, I did not recognize you. This horrible virus took you away. Dad, I wish I was there to hold your hand the way you were always there to hold my hand.

The world had to stop for you to earn your wings in heaven. You were simply too strong to leave us any other way. I wish I had spent more time with you. I wish I was able to talk to you more. I didn't know how to connect with you. I guess we were too much alike.

Dad, if there is one thing I can take away from this event, it's that you are a part of history. You are one of the number of lives that were taken due to COVID-19. You have left your mark on earth and you will forever be missed.

Thank you for never giving up on me and for always holding my hand.

I love you always,
Adrienne

~

Instead of consuming and digesting everything we see, read, and hear about this crisis on social media or the news, we can list just one thing we are grateful for, and if that feels good, we can do it again, and again, and again, as many times as we need to, until we're in a place where we feel gratitude. Then we can share our gratitude on social media and express how we cope with the crisis and let our positive experience become a model for someone else who is dealing with it.

For example, I'm grateful my grandma lives in a place where they temporarily stopped allowing visitors in for the time being to protect the health of the residents. I'm also grateful for telephones which allow me to talk with her, which is also a reminder that we are only as close or as far as one phone call away.

One way to feel like we have some control in a crisis is to help others. We can ask ourselves, *What is one small random act of kindness we could do for someone else with absolutely no expectation of anything in return?* Then we can be grateful for being able to help another.

ADVERSITY

by Shawn Davis

Dear God,

Thank you so much for the ADVERSITY in my life, both past and present. Adversity is a pivotal teacher of so many wonderful human attributes. Adversity teaches us about the human capacity for strength and perseverance. Adversity teaches us about courage and our heart's capacity to overcome our fears and anxiety to rise higher. Adversity can teach us about humility and ground us in the present moment. Adversity is the seasoning that gives victory such a sweet taste. Adversity is the spark or catalyst for character development. Last but certainly not least, adversity creates the opportunity to draw very close to you Father God. I have never felt closer to you or as "held" by you than when I face adversity that I cannot see how to overcome. Adversity strengthens our FAITH in you and reminds us that we can do all things THROUGH you. I am so grateful and appreciative of all that I have gained through the challenges and adversity that you have allowed in my life!

Gratefully yours...

Shawn Davis

Hope Radio Podcast

HILLIS'S STORY

by Hillis Pugh

My story is one of how I learned to be grateful. The spiritual path that I am now on started because of how I learned about gratitude through personal life experience. The foundation of gratitude was laid in the year 2006. It was in this year that I was laid off from my corporate job and had to find a new job. I took some time off before I began my search. I contemplated for a while what I wanted to do next in my life. There were underutilized skills and passions that had gone unexpressed. It was at this moment of contemplation that I decided to start my own marketing and graphic design business with a friend. This business was my livelihood; there was so much joy in tapping into a new sense of self. For two years, I helped small businesses see their value or the value of their products. It even pushed me beyond my limits. With the approach of 2008, I felt a shift in the economy and in my clients. Slowly my clients were lessening their involvement in my services, which, at the time, was considered a luxury for small businesses. I then took a part-time job to help supplement my income. The well was drying up and I didn't know what to do. Not only was the well drying up, but a romantic relationship was also ending. I felt all was crumbling around me with no clear way out.

Sunk into depression, I was barely making ends meet with my part-time job. The business was done, relationship over, rent due, and bills piling up. I was taught to find a way on my own, to make a way, but no one tells you that when you are in a low place, all you can see are mountains making it nearly impossible to reach them. I was full of pride. Somehow, I found a way to put my pride aside and summoned the courage to ask for help from family and friends.

Family always knows when you need help. When I asked my

family for financial help, it was given. At times it was given when not asked for, when they knew it was needed. I felt the tide turn in my favor. It was Thanksgiving 2008 when I learned the truth of gratitude.

Upon reflecting on 2008, I realize how important it is to put your pride aside and ask for help, but, most importantly, the love and support of family and friends to assist me emotionally and financially was invaluable. I was then able to see the same value in myself as I was showing my former clients. I learned that gratitude was not just a once-a-year event, that it could happen every day. When I woke the morning of Thanksgiving, I wrote a long email to my family and friends expressing my gratitude for their love and support in the past year. I didn't expect any response. Yet the responses I received moved me to tears. This was only the beginning of what was to come.

The responses I received motivated me to share more of what I was grateful for in my daily life. They helped me to seek out all that I was grateful for, everything from running water to finally getting a job. The expression of being grateful opened me up to feeling better in my life. I began to share email messages about what I was grateful for. I saw the little things in everyday life by giving power to them, all those little things once ignored.

By understanding the power of genuine gratitude, I learned that family, friends, and Source will always give something to be grateful for. See the gratitude in the everyday, as gratitude is just the foundation to much bigger things, as my own personal lessons have guided me to be a teacher, speaker, and author of gratitude.

MEETING THOMAS

"I had kept my gratitude locked up inside, as though it were a museum piece, rather than giving it back to its rightful owner."

Thomos Koulopoulos

I've met a lot of people during my gratitude journey. It's very easy to become fast friends with someone when you are speaking about gratitude and sharing personal stories about one's life. I was going to be interviewed on The Gratitude Podcast with Georgian Benta and I knew he'd ask me to share someone in my life I was grateful for. With this thought in mind I wanted to take this question a little deeper and add a second dimension to it. This idea came from a guest I listened to on Tim Ferriss's podcast years ago. One of Tim's go to questions at the time was who is the first person you think of when you hear the word successful? His guest said you know who most people will say and that really isn't that interesting. He went on to say what he would find more interesting is who you would think of second or third on that list. These ideas had been floating around in my head for several years. Then last week I figured a way to incorporate them.

At the beginning of my gratitude journey, when I wanted others to experience the feeling that I had received from writing the letter to my mom, I would seek out people posting anything and everything about gratitude on social media. Kevin Caldwell, author and motivational speaker, was one of the people I connected with on Twitter.

Kevin was so kind to be one of my guests on my short-lived podcast Liquid Gratitude. One day Kevin shot me a message with a link. It was a link to an Inc.com article titled "Do This For 30 Days and You Will Never Be The Same Again," by Thomas Koulopoulos. It is a really powerful piece of writing that you can read here:

I'd like to tell you a story. Stick with me. I promise it will be worth it and will forever change the way you think about your success in life and in business.

My high school sport was wrestling. It suited my personality of being both a team player and a fierce individual competitor. It's one of the most exhausting and emotionally demanding sports. You have no choice but to put every ounce of energy and concentration into what you're doing because your opponent is doing the same. For three two-minute periods there is no place to hide, no time to take a breath; every second is as intense as the last. In short, total physical and mental focus.

I was not an extraordinary wrestler. The vast majority of my opponents had more experience and were usually much larger. Even though I weighed in at 225 pounds, more than once I ended up under the crushing weight of a 275-pound opponent to the point of blacking out. Yes, to keep things fair, they do have weight classes in wrestling, but I was in the unlimited class. Trust me, upward of 250 pounds it's like talking about the wind-chill factor when the temperature is already 20 below zero -- it just doesn't matter any more.

Bridge!

However, I had a coach who refused to throw in the towel. Coach LeVasseur didn't know the meaning of giving up. As I was verging on passing out he'd cup his hands to his mouth and scream at me "Bridge!," a move you use when your back is against the mats, with your opponent on top. You arch your entire body, suspended by your feet and the back of your head. It's a last-ditch effort to stave off being pinned--the equivalent of a knockout in boxing.

"...it wasn't so much about winning as it was about not conceding defeat easily, about accepting that sometimes the best you can do is fight like hell and accept it gracefully."

The lessons I learned from those years stuck with me in so many ways. The notion that going back, meet after meet, to give it my all was everything; it wasn't so much about winning as it was about not conceding defeat easily, about accepting that sometimes the best you can do is fight like hell and accept it gracefully. Good lesson, but not the most important lesson. That one would come about 35 years later.

A voice from the past

My son, Adam, had taken up wrestling when he was 12. I was proud to see him learning the same lessons I had learned. Halfway through Adam's first season he came down with a nasty flu. I made a midnight run to pick up some meds for him. It was the middle of December and the only 24/7 pharmacy was empty and just happened to be one I didn't frequent often. As I walked in I heard someone call out my name from behind me. I hadn't seen coach LeVasseur for 35 years and yet that voice was unmistakable. "Coach Lev?," I said, with a sense of disbelief. We shook hands and I reached out to give him a hug. I thought to myself, "Had he always been shorter than me?" We chatted for a bit and I remembered that he had twin daughters who were his pride and joy. He'd talk about them endlessly during our brutal workouts. It was this odd mix of drill sergeant and devoted dad that made Lev so endearing. I asked how they were. His look changed suddenly. I could see the face that had always been lit by a fire of deep passion and caring turn to sorrow.

He looked me square in the eyes, "We lost Elise in a car accident years ago." My heart sank to the floor. What could I possibly say? I struggled to find something comforting. I told him I was sorry, that I remembered how often he'd talk about both of his daughters. He thanked me but the sadness cut through me. The whole time his eyes never glanced away. Coach Lev always looked you in the eyes.

It was at that moment when I realized that in more than 35 years I had never thanked him. I had thought about how I attributed so much of my success to him and that mental image of his booming voice yelling "Bridge!" whenever I'd feel the crushing weight of competitors, naysayers, and life's many challenges trying to pin my shoulders to the mats.

"I had kept my gratitude locked up inside, as though it were a museum piece, rather than giving it back to its rightful owner."

I said the only thing I could think of: "You know, Coach, I should have told you this a long time ago but I owe you so much for what you taught me, what you taught so many of us. I'm grateful for that, always will be. You touched countless lives. Thank you."

The experience felt surreal. The timing of it, with Adam having just *started wrestling, my own life in limbo after having sold my business, the contrast to the joy of the season, and the chance one-in-a-million encounter.*

But what struck me most was the realization and the shame of not having thanked Coach Lev earlier. I had kept my gratitude locked up inside, as though it were a museum piece, rather than giving it back to its rightful owner.

The gratitude challenge

As I drove home I started going down the long list of other people who had shaped me: my junior high gym teacher, who didn't give up on a very overweight 13-year-old until he could run a seven minute mile; the college professor who started me on my tech career; my first boss, who helped me start my first business by letting me use his office space and equipment for a full year; mentors, friends, relatives; so many people I owed so much to and yet had never expressed gratitude to directly.

So, are you getting the lesson yet? Yes, it's a simple one, gratitude: showing it, saying it, and sharing it.

Since that chance encounter I've tried to take some time out every few days to tell someone I'm grateful for what they've done to help me personally and professionally. Trust me, it's a list that never ends -- not for any of us.

If you're successful, driven, confident, it's because people believed in you when you likely didn't believe in yourself.

So, for the next 30 days, do something transformational: I call it the Gratitude Challenge. Make a list of 30 people you are grateful to and each day send a short note/email/txt -- heck, maybe even an actual call -- to each of them. No need for great eloquence. Say it simply and directly. Start today, right now, as soon as you're done reading this. The great irony in life is that we most often fail to recognize and thank those closest to us, the ones who have shaped us most. We carry that gratitude inside of us but rarely express it directly to them. And guess what? You need to hear your-self say it.

At the end of 30 days I guarantee you that two things will happen: you will never again underestimate the power of expressing simple gratitude, and you will find many more opportunities to pay it forward. And that will forever change the way you live your life and run your business.

As for coach Lev, I found out that just a few months after losing his daughter, he took on the then-vacant position of coaching the girls' varsity track and field team, taking it from one of the worst teams in the state to one of the most successful. After 35 years he was still coaching me on how to be grateful.

So, what are you waiting for?

After reading this article, I was speechless. This guy got it. Not only did he get it but I wanted to get a letter from him. At the time I was all about the letters. The letters were my gateway to sparking these moments of gratitude. I went on to read more about him and check out his website. The first thing that sprung off the page at me was a quote by Steve Wozniak, the co-founder of Apple Computer, that read, "That was the best presentation I've ever heard - including all of the Ted Talks I've been to." I noticed that he had released several books that were translated into many languages and sold hundreds of thousands of copies. I sent him a tweet that read: "A friend just shared your article on gratitude. Really amazing stuff. Would you be open to collaborating on a gratitude project?" He messaged me back later that day and at 7:30pm that night, on May 26, 2015, we talked on the phone.

Thomas became my friend, mentor, and savior in one instant. I can honestly say that without his encouragement, belief, and love, this book would not exist.

Who is a person in your life that has given you a similar experience? Have you shared your gratitude with them? If not, why haven't you?

I went to New York on the second anniversary of my mom's passing to host Gratitude New York. I was walking around, near

Times Square, one early morning. I met Joe and Carl, two African American men in their fifties or sixties. I don't remember exactly how we started talking. They must have asked me for money or something because I remember asking them what they really wanted. Carl said that he really wanted some new shoes. I didn't have enough money to buy him shoes. As for my own shoes, well I was wearing them and I just couldn't give them up.

I offered to buy them coffee or a sandwich from the Times Square McDonald's, so we headed that way. As we walked together, I learned that Carl had just been released from prison that morning. Joe had met him and was supposed to take him to his apartment, but Joe's girlfriend was fighting with him and wasn't having it. This had left Joe and Carl walking the streets in the middle of the night, penniless.

At McDonald's, one ordered a coffee and the other a breakfast sandwich. It was a pleasant morning. We talked about gratitude. Carl was so in his head that he asked me what he had to be grateful for. I took a beat and said, "Well you aren't in prison." Carl and Joe both laughed, and Carl admitted, "Yeah, you are right." It's amazing how stuck we can be in our heads. This can easily happen to all of us. For Carl, something as massive as not being locked up anymore had escaped his attention and his gratitude. This man didn't have a home. He had gotten out of prison only to find out that the place he was going to stay wasn't happening. That disappointment had made him forget that he was free. It had made him totally disconnected from his gratitude. I told him, "Gratitude is like your breath. You need to connect to it. You've got it; it's always there. Appreciate it. Live it." After we talked, I gave them money for the subway so they could go to Joe's place, hoping that the girlfriend would allow Carl to stay.

I know that I've lived a very fortunate life. I know this, and I still forget about it. It's possible to walk around in a grateful state and still forget this simple fact. Let's start with the fact that I have already won the lottery of life. Out of millions of sperms, somehow that one sperm made it to the egg, and I was born. The odds were not stacked in my favor. That's true for all of us who have been given the gift of life.

AN EXPERIMENT

"It's a funny thing about life, once you begin to take note of the things you are grateful for, you begin to lose sight of the things that you lack."

Germany Kent

I've been reading the book *30 Days of Gratitude: Daily Gratitude Exercises to Uplift Your Thoughts and Improve Your Life* by Wendy Bett. Yesterday's experiment was about color. I had to make a conscious decision of what my favorite color is. It's blue. Then I had to think of all the things that are blue that are pleasing to me. These can be anything: my car, my notebook, my backpack. In my case, it's the sky, the ocean, my dad's eyes. Next, I simply had to go about my day looking for that color. Whenever I saw it, I said *thank you*.

Looking for blue and expressing gratitude upon each discovery is simple. It's an easy starting point. I did the experiment. I ended up thinking about and seeing blue throughout my day. Every time I saw blue, I simply said to myself *thank you*. My watch band was blue... *Thank you*. Someone's shirt was blue... *Thank you*.

This experiment is quite powerful for several reasons. First, it makes our day memorable. Most days are a flash of nothing. We get up, drive to work, work, go home, have dinner, watch television, go to sleep. Actively looking for something and saying thank you throughout the day makes it different. Second, this thought exercise makes us present and brings us into the moment. The moment is where we want to be. It's all there truly is. The past is gone, and the future is not here yet. Gratitude is all about appreciating the present moment, appreciating what is here now.

A.J. Jacobs, who has also been interviewed on GratitudeSpace, is the author of *Thanks a Thousand*. Here's an excerpt of his book:

Since I'm doing a project on gratitude, I figure I'd better practice some thankfulness to try to calm myself down. So as I stand on the platform, I remind myself of this fact: Just as hundreds of things must go right for my coffee to exist, I've also had hundreds of things go right for me today.

For starters:

I did not trip on the subway stairs and break my collarbone.

The elevator in my building did not plummet to the basement and give me a concussion.

My fare card had enough money on it to get me through the turnstile, which didn't stick when I pushed it.

The key is to remind myself that I'm a lucky bastard. To make a concerted effort to acknowledge all the good things I take for granted. To battle my brain's built-in negative bias, the one that might have helped our Paleo ancestors avoid predators but that often puts me in a miserable mood.

Yes, I missed the train today, but what about all the times I got to the subway platform just as the doors were opening, allowing me to slip into the car while suppressing a smug smile? The reality is, I'm not unlucky with subways—it just seems that way because the enraging experiences are the ones that stick in my memory. It's the same distorted way that I process feedback. If I get one hundred compliments and one insult, what do I remember?

The insult.

Fighting this bias requires an active strategy. A commitment to noticing. The next time I'm in a drugstore line that moves quickly, or am assigned an airport gate located right next to security instead of a half-mile walk past frozen yogurt shops, I vow to actually point out my good fortune to myself. I'll even say it out loud: "I'm grateful this line was so short!" Maybe that'll get it through my thick, biased skull.

I've become a fan of a mental game I call "It could be worse." It can be a creative little exercise. I think to myself: The subway signs are confusing, but at least they're in English, not Latvian. The subway platform is depressing, but at least there's no one singing "Bohemian Rhapsody" next to an open guitar case.

I recently read an article about the poet Robert Bly, who said that when he was a kid and skinned his knee, his mother would say, "Just be thankful that you didn't break your leg." He found it annoying at the time, which is understandable. But he now sees its perverse wisdom.

"Being grateful to me is never failing to look for the light...despite the dark."

Shawn Anderson (taken from interview on GratitudeSpace)

In times of crisis it's important to appreciate our surroundings. I saw a funny post on Facebook about staying safe during the pandemic that read, "Your grandparents had to go off to war; all you have to do is stay in your home." It's true. We have got it so good living in a modern society. It's hard to even fathom how different life was just a few generations ago. Most of today's complaints are related to the conveniences of our modern society. *I can't get a signal! My flight's been delayed! They don't have this or that brand at the grocery store! My package is coming tomorrow instead of today!* We live in an instant gratification world. Unfortunately, all this instant gratification has left us ungrateful.

It's important to look at things from a different perspective and appreciate them on a different level.

POVERTY

by Brandy M. Miller

Dubbed "relentlessly positive" by William Hung, international speaker and award-winning author Brandy M. Miller specializes in opportunity prospecting and the cultivation of underdeveloped human beings.

As strange as it may sound, I am so grateful for the forty plus years I spent living in poverty. Most of those years, I thought poverty was my enemy. I fought it every way that I could, and I kept failing. It wasn't until 2012 that I began to look at Poverty in a new light. I saw it as a teacher, patient but strict, who was showing me things about myself that I needed to know. Poverty taught me to be creative, to be resilient, and to begin to understand that my value was not in my bank account but in the service that I could render to others and the way that I could work to change the lives of those around me for the better.

If not for my experiences with poverty, I would not have published The Poverty Diaries in 2014. If not for the Poverty Diaries, I would not have come to understand that everything I went through during those years was not done to me but allowed for me in order to transform me into the person I needed to become to make the difference in the world that I was born to make.

I am rich beyond measure no matter what is, or is not, in my bank account because I know the value of the gifts and talents I have to offer the world, and I use those to make the world a better place for my having been here.

I leave you with this passage from the book:
Stuff for Sale
Read me a book just the other day

Taught me to see things a whole new way
Said my problems were just opportunities
If I could only learn to change the way I see
So I counted up my assets like it said to do
Here's what I found I can offer to you:
I've got 30 paintings that I can't sell
A car in the driveway that's broke as hell
Seventy-five thousand dollars in debt
A college degree that ain't paid off yet
One sterling silver necklace a friend gave to me
And 39 years experience in poverty
Well, I scratched my head at the bits I'd found
But I didn't quit yet, the advice seemed sound
It told me to keep a tally, and to take measure
Of all the things I found, my hidden treasure
So I counted up my assets like it said to do
Here's a few more things I can offer you:
I've got a voice like an angel, you can order to go
I can write you a song or a poem or a book,
You know I can teach you to paint or to draw, if you please
I can speak to a large group or small with great ease
I can offer a couch to the wealthy who seek
A unique experience living poor for $5000 a week
I was feeling much better
As I wrote down this letter
All I needed now was people who'd pay
A little money goes a very long way
And maybe this story's ending'll be sweet
If only someone will buy the things I can sell.

NONNA (MAY 9, 1909 - FEBRUARY 9, 2002)

by Carmin Caterina

Carmin Caterina is the Founder of Lessons For My Daughters.

Eighteen years ago, I lost my real-life angel, my nonna Caterina. She was truly the biggest light in my life growing up.

She was really magical. She was the first to teach me about life beyond the physical and other realms. She would tell me about the spirits that would visit her at the edge of her bed at night. She often spoke of death and being reunited with her husband who had passed many years prior, but she told me she couldn't leave unless she knew I was ok.

I don't know if Nonna knew of the pain and abuse I was living at home while she was here in the flesh, but she knew that I needed her protection. I wonder if that was why she treated me like I was the most important thing in the world when we were together. Nonna would tell me my eyes were like the stars in the sky, and I believed her.

Nonna refused to give up her home even though each one of her children offered that she come live with them. She was fiercely independent and made it clear that the moment she wasn't she would leave this place. Nonna would still walk to church every day at the age of 92.

She would often fall, and the last time she did, she ended up in the hospital and was told she needed to go through rehabilitation to learn to walk again. They felt she was too old for surgery and her heart would not survive the anesthesia.

The last time I saw her I told her that I was going to get married and that I wanted her to be at my wedding. She said "si dio vuole" which means "if God wants." I didn't realize that I would never see her again.

She had told my mother in the hospital that she would never be getting out of the bed again, that she would never walk again, and she was right. Her words had power. She never made it to the rehabilitation center.

I was planning to go with my mom to visit her that day, to take her some clothes. I went to the mall with a friend in the morning while my mom was working in the garden, and we were planning to go later. While I was at the mall, we took a break to eat. I felt this wave of sadness come over me, and I started to cry, but I didn't know why.

I got the call while I was standing in the middle of Macy's, and the world stood still just for a moment. I told her I was getting married the last time I saw her. She knew someone else would be taking care of me. She could no longer be independent, and she wanted no part of that.

I was completely devastated and heartbroken, but I was also happy for her because she got what she wanted. She went into cardiac arrest and was successfully revived only to leave again. She knew what she wanted and what she did not, and no one could change that.

Our connection feels divine in so many ways. I know she was here in part to make sure I made it and my light could see its way through the darkness. She was that mirror and reflection for me. There's so much I would ask her if she were still here: Did she have moments of fear where she didn't feel so in control of her life and her destiny?

As Nonna got older I thanked God every night for one more day with her because I knew how lucky I was to have her in my life for so long. I knew she wouldn't be here forever, yet she lives through me still. She's the reason I strive to be the light for others and, in that way, her love will last forever.

Eighteen years and I feel all the pain of that day. I miss you so much, Nonna, and I know your love carries me through the hard times, even today.

MOM'S EULOGY

by Elizabeth de la Portilla

Elizabeth de la Portilla is a retired anthropology professor living in Italy, learning to live in a world outside of a classroom. She is a wife and keeper of cats. She misses her mom dearly and wears red lipstick in her honor.

I cannot be with you today, but my beloved niece and travel buddy, Elizabeth Claire, is kind enough to read this for me. She and our other nieces and nephews have known their grandparents, and to know one's grandparents is a gift beyond measure.

I believe within a family each sibling experiences a different set of parents. Each of us share similar ideas, beliefs of who and what our parents are, and then there are details unique to each of us because of time and circumstances. My earliest memories of mom are café con leche, Captain Kangaroo, and her making tortillas. On the kitchen floor of our house in a corner where the counter and stove meet, the yellow linoleum is worn nearly white, the grooved patterns erased by the many hours she spent shuffling between the counter rolling out tortillas and the hot comal on her right. I would sit at the kitchen table doing homework and watch as Daddy came up behind Mom and put his arm around her waist while she cooked.

My dad often touched my mom, her arm, her back, her butt. He called her reina, she called him "honey." He brought her coffee every morning as I lay in the other room half awake. I can still hear him sit on the edge of the bed, she is stirring the coffee, spoon bell-like against the china, as they plan the day. This is love, this is how I believed married people were. Imagine my surprise the first morning I woke up, as a wife, and saw Johnny standing at the edge of our bed, no coffee. It took him years to learn. Thank you, Mom, and Dad.

Daddy was larger than life and Mom was a force of nature. To me, there was no one more beautiful than my mother and she had the best legs God ever gave a woman. She dressed in a sense of style, way ahead of her time; in shades of color that heightened her beauty. And the shoes! Can we take a moment for the shoes? Stilettos, flats, kitten heels, block heels, leather, reptile, vinyl, and purses to match! Don't get me started on her jewelry or scarves or the importance of red lipstick. I grew to appreciate my inner girl late in life and Paris only reinforces what my mom taught me. True style is about confidence and carriage; Mom had both in abundance.

I often wondered how Mom could afford such beautiful clothes when we were so poor. I mean we didn't starve or anything, but how did she do it? My brother Virgil finally provided the answer: She was an excellent seamstress. Then I remembered the junior high prom dress she made for me, pink with sheer sleeves and lace across the bodice, and our summer vacation clothes with head scarves to match; she could sew anything; just ask Virgil about his Halloween costumes. And her cooking!

How many of us remember our moms in the kitchen with amagrande sitting at the table, everybody making tamales? Fifty, sixty, seventy dozens. She hated the way I spread masa, so she put me to soak the hojas, Diane laughing at me, because she could spread masa. Tommy was outside, he and Danny Gonzalez getting into trouble, like always. Mom and the tias, coming together after work drinking coffee and eating pan dulce while reaffirming family, being able to relax, with time to themselves before dinner and husbands. Tia Kate has a shy laugh, but Tia Lupe's was sly and bawdy. I loved hearing their laughter. Mom wanted her sisters around her always. And I soaked up the lessons like a sponge.

Henry Peña remembers when we all went to Grandma's house at seven every evening to pray the rosary. What I remember is running around in the yard with the younger cousins throwing nueces at one another, huge pecans from the giant tree in her yard. Amagrande would gather us all up on the big porch and tell us stories about Mexico and the revolution. Who needed Netflix when we had our grandmother?

And that is the point, "when we had our grandmother." The years have been cruel; we have lost nearly all our matriarchs. One by one, the links to our past are being broken. But we embody their dreams and desires; we reflect lessons learned. All of us, de Leons, Peñas, Hernandez, Portillas are survivors; our parents were survivors; we are survivors. Our generation are the teachers now. What are the lessons we teach? What will we leave behind?

Aida and Virgil are teachers for my nieces and nephews, and their compassion and unending loving service to our mother as dementia erased her being is a testament to our parents, our grandparents, and all those who have passed before us. Our better angels, incarnate. Thank you, mana and mano.

One last story. When I was in high school, we had an assignment, to bring a cultural example of food into class. Well on the day mine was due, I was empty handed; mom said she was going to bring something to class and not to worry. So, when the time came, mom and the tias walked in with paper plates of enchiladas de chile y queso, rice, and beans, more than thirty plates total. The teacher stood there with her mouth open; she had expected a sample--but never underestimate the pride of Mexican mothers. We all chowed down and drank Big Red. Sometimes the best example of family love is a plate of enchiladas.

Overly generous, caring, complicated, beautiful, a diva, loyal, loving, tireless, Maria de Leon de la Portilla, my mom, our mom, was all these things. As I get older, when I look in the mirror, I see more and more of her in my face. I hope she is proud of me. Thank you, Mom. I love you always.

LIFE LESSONS

by Diane Riley

Diane Riley is a former journalist, proofreader, and copy editor. Her favorite thing in the whole wide world is reading; researching comes in at a close second. She is currently writing her first novel.

The water in the cove, stirred by the early morning's breeze, shows off nature's version of impressionism. Trees and rocks are mirrored but ragged. The colors are true—gray greens and brown greens, gray-brown trunks—but splotchy. Two kayaks, one orange with a man and a young boy as passengers, one blue and white with a woman and another boy, further disturb the water as they glide into the cove.

A kayak comes ashore, and the father and boy climb out. The boy has become a frog-hunter. Farther away, his older sibling is taking the in-the-kayak hunting approach. His mother steers the kayak quietly below the low branches, into the dark places where frogs are known to hide. In and out. In and out. Now you see the kayak, now you don't. The younger boy calls out, "Mamma, come here. I've found something." She answers that she'll be there soon.

...

Earlier this morning, before the kayaks arrived, I met a family of ducks, a mother and seven ducklings. They came up to the grassy area where I was sitting, looking for breakfast bugs. The mom kept her eyes on me as they all ate. After a while she herded her babies back into the water. They swam around a bit, getting very close to the dam and small waterfall. Then the mother decided it was time to jump over the dam and waterfall, into the brook below.

She headed off, down the brook, quacking. One duckling

jumped, landed in the crest of the waterfall, and made it into the brook. The other ducklings peeped excitedly for a bit as they swam around, and then five more jumped over the dam. One was still not going for it. As his mother called him, he peeped and swam. What to do? What to do? I sensed he might need a bit of encouragement, so I walked over. The mother saw my movement and quacked loudly. The duckling looked at me and down he went, through the falls. All seven accounted for, they paddled away with the mother.

...

Now, the two frog hunters are cheering victorious, each claiming a bullfrog. In their celebration, a kayak tips, a boy screams, the mom calls out. But dad is in the water too. He tries to get the boy back into the kayak, but the boy is more concerned about his lost bullfrog. Eventually the boy is put back into the kayak, and the dad pushes it to shore and gets back in. Everyone is calm. Life-jackets are on. No one is hurt. A nice learning experience for the kids: Here's how you get back into a kayak if you tip over. If you can't get back in, here's how you push it to the nearest shore. After the life lesson, the kayakers quietly paddle away.

Just as they leave, the duck family returns. I hear the mother calling and the ducklings peeping before I see them walking the path worn down by anglers, between a black birch and stone wall. They waddle across the grass landing, back into the cove.

The duck returns her family to the stone dam, and all eight sit to enjoy the sun. Suddenly, two of the ducklings decide to jump the dam and waterfall. The mother squawks and jumps after them, leaving the other five ducklings on the dam. The mother herds the two ducklings in the brook while the other five pace and peep on the dam. One heads for the grassy area across from the dam, the others following. I worry they will go into the nearby road. I run over a small wooden bridge and herd the ducklings back to the stonewall that edges the brook.

I hear the mother quacking below in the bushes. One duckling on the stonewall jumps and four run away. The four return to the wall, two jump in, and two run away. It's like watching a nursery rhyme. Then two come back, one jumps, one pauses and then jumps. I'm hoping they all made it.

Ten minutes later, back at the landing, the duck returns with one, two, three, four, five, six, seven ducklings. Yay! They all made it. Then she brings them back to the dam wall. This must be duck school, I realize. She again jumps into the brook. This time all but one follow, some more hesitant than others. The one that doesn't jump repeatedly runs from the edge of the dam and back again. It jumps into the water and tries to swim over the dam but backs off. It gets on the grass landing and I herd it back. It jumps back into the cove and swims around. During this time, the mother has been quacking rather calmly. The duckling crosses over to the other grassy side and I head for the wooden bridge again, wanting to keep it from the road. Before I can make it to the bridge, the duckling finds the spot on the stonewall where it and four siblings had jumped, and it makes the dive.

Then it clicks. A nice learning experience for ducklings: This is how you get away from something going after you in the cove. You head for the brook. You can go over the waterfall, over the dam itself, or go to the side and jump over the other wall. And here's how you get back to the cove. You take this trail created by anglers over the years . . . No one's injured, everyone made it to the brook all three times.

All this took place within an hour or so. As I sit and reflect, I am filled with gratitude that the duck was willing to trust me nearby as she taught her ducklings one of their life lessons, just as the parents had with their children earlier. Animals and humans: we're more alike than we realize.

PERSISTENCE

by Ifumi Ehigiator

Ifumi Ehigiator is a Nigerian writer and poet.

I watch her struggle to pull herself up and she falls back to the ground. She does this till she successfully stands, regardless of how many times she has attempted the feat. She holds on to an object which poses as a support to her. Her attitude, even when she fails to reach her goal, is formidable. She could just turn in your direction and render an innocent and hopeful smile, exposing her toothless gum. The challenge at hand leaves her unperturbed. She is my little seven-month-old baby. By watching her, I have been able to understand the power of persistence. I understand that persistence can unlock any door. Persistence is complemented by focus. The next time I am tempted to lose focus, I'll remember my little girl.

LETTER TO GRATITUDE

by Sasha Michael

Dear Gratitude,

It's me, Sasha. I know it's been a while since I've written to update you on my life, but I know you can tell things have gotten so much better since I started listening to you. I know you won't say "I told you so," but I definitely know you did!

I know the last time we connected I was still struggling to make it a practice to be thankful. I started small as you suggested, thinking about just the things around me: the roof over my head, the food on the table, the clean water to drink; how nice it is having clothes on my back, and that cute top I got on sale is awesome too. I'm thankful for that cup of coffee that makes my weekends so much better and for the energy I get from drinking and enjoying it. I checked in with my feelings, and you were right: I felt better.

The days went on, and I started to be thankful for so much more. I would express thanks for my wonderful family and friends. I quickly noticed that any triggered feeling or upset from certain people had dissolved away, just like you said it would. The hurt or pain I once felt in my heart over certain situations no longer felt in alignment with holding space in my heart. You encouraged me to let go and make room for more. I am so glad you did.

From there, I really grew to love being grateful for even bigger intangible things, like my ability to keep learning, to stay positive in tough times, and being able to express my emotions so clearly. The more I noticed, the more I saw. Then, one day, it just became something I did every day, without much effort. In fact, every morning, I wake up and it's the first thing I think about! Thank you for that.

I remember all those times you tried to show me that things would get better if I only changed my perspective. I know I didn't believe you for years, and you patiently waited for me to finally grasp it, that no matter how old we are, we have the choice to learn new habits that make us fall in love with life again, fall in love with ourselves again. I know I was quite stuck at one time, and I appreciate that you stayed alongside me and never gave up on me. I have been able to put everything I am doing into practice with my daughter, and I am delighted to say she has been taking to it beautifully.

I wanted you to know that while you aren't expecting me to show my appreciation for you, I always do and will. You've changed my life experience for the better, and I truly can't thank you enough. Although, most of all, I wanted to thank you for teaching me the most important person to be grateful for is myself. Without me, there wouldn't be you.

I remain ever grateful for us both.

With Love,

Sasha

~

It's easy to get frustrated when an inconvenience occurs. For most, it's the first natural reaction. Getting frustrated won't make anyone feel better, though. Besides, it will take time and effort to undo that feeling and replace it with a positive or happy one. Having a different perspective will allow for positivity from the start. It may take some practice with gratitude. Instead of focusing on the inconvenience, feeling thankful and even excited for all the positive aspects of a situation will keep the person feeling happy. Continuing to concentrate on the good will create a continuous feeling of gratitude and happiness.

MOMENTS

by D

Is it bizarre to be grateful for the moments in our lives that caused us or others pain? Moments that still stick with us so profoundly that there isn't a year that goes by when something in our present doesn't suddenly re-color that shattered part of our past?

As I recollect on where I am now, living a life that I strive to have filled with action, passion, purpose, and love, instead of regret, I cannot think of a single thing I've learned because of beauty. Everything I've learned has been only of fear, tragedy, or consequence.

My parents met while my dad was a professor and my mother a student. My mother quit college and moved back home to work. If not for a car accident that caused her terminal back pain, I would not have been born. My dad sent her a note saying he needed her. He got divorced before his wife left him. And therefore I exist.

My dad was 40 when he had me, way older than my other friends' parents. I swore at a young age I'd work harder, faster, and smarter to achieve what I wanted in life so he would still be alive to see that. He was, and is still thriving. I live knowing he's proud of me and an active part of what I do.

When I was in 6th grade, I got sick. No one knew what it was. I developed a fear of needles for months. I didn't learn how to socialize and was the "sick kid." It gave me a distorted view of reality I never escaped, like being able to run a 7-min mile and thinking I was still overweight. The photos don't show that, but my memory lies to me every day.

If our memory is informed by emotion, by trauma, can we trust it to guide us, or do we need to develop perspective and practices to counter ourselves? I did.

From this experience I developed a resolve that is indefatigable. I can work through immense exhaustion and pain, shrugging it off to achieve what I want, and my sense of humor carries me through all of it.

I quit classical piano a year later, and only got back into it because of grunge rock. I started to improvise and then compose, creating a path for my inner emotions that has lasted 29 years and counting as a composer.

When I face a-holes in my life, people who threaten my ability to do my work or insult me, I know they can never take my music away from me. They can't take away my gift, so they can't take away my integrity.

Socialization remained humiliating in high school. I never let on because I developed a stoicism in my reactions, except when I was acting or playing piano, which led me to a gradual then sudden launch in my career, working for people where I couldn't show my emotion or disdain for how they treated others. I thrived and they came around to my strategy, and our shared success.

But I never realized that not fitting into any one group would be my superpower. I was always in-between.

So I stayed that way, being an exceptional judge of character (except in dating—until I met my wife) and someone who could maintain hundreds of relationships with empathy, before empathy was a "common term" because I only cared about motivating others so that they felt heard, and because I believed they could do more to awaken their passions through meeting other like-minded people.

This became its own side business, both fueling my daily work and fueling my soul.

I am grateful because of my mother quitting college, getting into a car accident, my dad getting divorced to marry my mom, getting sick and nearly "dying," learning that my perception of my self is always partly false, leaving piano only to come back in my own way and to define my life as an artist, having a hard time socializing and fitting in, and therefore being able to hold my emotions back in order to give someone else the space to share their own.

Gratitude is a tricky beast. If we're grateful for what we've become, do we want it to come from compliments and expressions that we then shrug off because we know we shouldn't be so proud of who we are? Do we want it to come from lessons learned that still haunt us?

I am grateful that I learned early on that no one sees my journey as fully as myself, that life cannot be linear and the only time I should be proud I walked a straight line is if I'm drunk, that we repeat to ourselves what we know until we believe it to be truth, that we realize that there is no one "truth" to understanding our journey, that the beauty of life is in the journey itself and how our lives intersect with others' at moments outside of our control.

~

The one-year anniversary of my mom's passing was coming up and I wanted to make it special. I had people write letters of love to my mom and share stories and memorable events. I made this day special for myself as well. I got up early and went to Starbucks to work on the site. Every hour for fifteen hours, I posted a new letter of love people had written for my mom. These letters have been captured as they were written with no editing or grammar changes.

LETTERS TO MY MOM

OUR LAST DAY TOGETHER

ONE OF THE BEST DAYS OF MY LIFE

by Krystle Gossett

It started a week prior to our last day together.

My family and I were leaving to go to the Goetz Condo in Ft. Myers later Friday night and I got the text from Al to pray hard for you as you were being admitted into the hospital. I asked the Lord if I should come and it was so clear that I should. We decided I was going to surprise you at the hospital. Todd, the kids, and my parents would pick me up in Louisville late that night on their way to FL. The look on your face was priceless when I arrived at the hospital. Our tears of joy to see each other spoke a thousand words. You were so frustrated that Al let you take the meds to help you sleep (him knowing that I was coming). Everyone left the room to give the 2 of us some time to chat and out of nowhere you started feeling sick. We laughed hard after the fact, but the Lord as always knew the desires of your heart...you got sick and threw up the 3 little blue pills (sleeping meds) and said, "Well, what in the world...I don't remember eating any blue M&M's today?!" We laughed later too at that comment and soon you realized we would get to spend the next hour together after all instead of you sleeping It was a very special hour. We talked about all types of things and before I left I hugged you so tight as I prayed for you! Before I left the hospital I told you I would see you in one week, but the next time would be at YOUR house! You were quite the woman of strength and with determination I knew you'd get back home!

I left for a week in Florida with my family and we stayed in close contact through text. Your family took such great care of you and one of your besties and sisters in Christ, Tonya, came to help take care of you too! Fast forward to Sunday when I came back to Louisville on our way home.... my family continued home, but I came to your house to spend the day with you at HOME! That day is a day I will NEVER forget and will forever cherish! We went on a walk (Jeannie, Al, you, and I) through your pretty neighborhood and as we pushed you in the wheelchair you looked like a diva wearing your sunglasses Pretty as ever! What a blessing it was for me to FINALLY get to meet your sweet daughter, Jeannie! It was as if I had known her for years. You asked to spend some time with just me. As we sat rocking in your sun room I will never forget all the wisdom you poured into me that day. We laughed, we cried, and we laughed more. It was some of your best last hours on this earth and I reminisce back to those hours so often. As I continue to lead my Shaklee team I constantly think of YOU and try so hard to lead with love, passion, and grace as you did! Your joy was a ray of sunshine and hope to everyone you met and I am honored to be your Shaklee daughter!

I MISS YOU BEYOND WORDS! Our time together was way too short on this earth, but I look forward to the day where we do a happy dance together at the feet of our Lord and Savior! Happy 1 Year Homecoming Sweet Shaklee Mama!

LAURA, I MISS YOU

by Erica Ladden

I miss seeing your sweet smile shine from across the room. I am so grateful for the short amount of time I had with you. You were always strengthening me in my walk, speaking life over my circumstances, and just being full of love. Your heart was always good. Your laugh was contagious, and you were one of the prettiest ladies I have known. Thank you for loving me into this family so well. I love you and I know you are dancing with Jesus everyday!!!

I LOVE MY AMERICAN GRANDMA!

by Warisara Changkaew

Dear grandma,

You're the most loving, generous, and caring person I have ever known. I still remember the first day I met you. I was really excited to see you and grandpa! You smiled at me and said, "Hi". You also gave me a welcome hug. And then I gave you the souvenir from Thailand. I was so happy when you said you loved it! You took me to survey the house. You played piano and we sang together. We sang Amazing grace, Joy to the world and Happy birthday song. I love your singing grandma! You have such a wonderful voice.You made me so happy and joyful. I love the way you think! I love the way you acted toward grandpa.

It showed me that love is real.

I love the way you treated your son and daughter. It showed me how much you love and care for them.

I love the way you acted to me. It showed me that how much you love me. Grandma...I still keep the Christmas gift you gave me. It makes me think of you when I look at it.

Thank you so much, grandma, for always making me laugh and happy.

Thank you god for letting me know such a great person like you.

Those special memories of you will always bring a smile. I will always remember you. You are in my heart always. I love you so much!

Your Thai niece,

Warisara Changkaew

TO LAURA

From Tanya Ladden

Time.... I have often thought clouds mimic time. You see them passing... silent... sometimes they rush by... sometimes they move so slowly you think they are standing still. Sometimes they are soft and billowy or full of thunder...

That is what this year has been like since you went to be with Jesus. Moments seemed to stand still, then I look back and it's been a year!

You would be so proud of your family. In the depth of their grief, they have lived. They, each finding their path, and growing in love and understanding of each other. You are ever present... each of them are finding a strength and new missions... and I see your reflection.

I wonder, often, about what you are doing... It must be so Grand! Singing and praising the Lord, walking with Him in the Garden...enjoying those you met at the Gate....being in His continual Presence... a place where there is no time...Ahaaaa

Your legacy is rippling into a new generation, and I know God smiles....

I miss your Sister- friendship

I treasure our time.

I miss your wisdom...

MOM

by Your Blessed Daughter, Jeannie

Mom,

I am not sure when you are in heaven if you know anything going on here!

It has been a big year without you present. But I must say your spirit is always strong around me! I praise the Lord there are no regrets between us. We lived our relationship to the fullest as mother + daughter + best friends.

I would want you to know dad and Chris have done so good. Don't get me wrong they have missed you every single day, but they are living with purpose and carrying your spirit.

There have been great testimonies you would be so happy and full of joy! You planted so many seeds in our lives and we are experiencing the harvest.

We celebrate your spirit and we will see you again when our assignment is done here. I know you will be the first person at heaven's gate welcoming us in!

Your blessed daughter, Jeannie
Your legacy carries on.

A TOUCH OF LOVE

by Tammy Meyers

Dear Laura,

I only had the pleasure of knowing you for a few years. But, it is a time of my life I will never forget.

The way you loved life, people, health, and God blew me away every time I had the blessing of being in your presence. At a time in my life when I was deeply wracked with grief, you reminded me of how much God loved me, that He never had and never would leave my side. You spoke truth over my life, allowed God to use you to breathe HIS LIFE back into my weary spirit. You built me up, taught me to fight the enemy, and rejoiced with me at each moment of victory. You prayed for me. Laura, when I look back at this time, there is one powerful memory that always returns. I was visiting from out of town and slept in your guest room. It was early in the morning and I had just gotten up. You came into the room with your cheerful, beautiful smile and hugged me, saying good morning and how happy you were that I was there. It might sound silly, but that hug reached right into my soul and reminded me of God's compassionate, tender love for me. You didn't see the tears that welled up as I received the love God was giving me through you. You didn't know the depth of comfort I felt, having just lost both parents, to feel that touch of love wrap around my sadness and warm my spirit. To you, it was just another morning of you doing what you do. But, to me, it was one of the first moments I remember FEELING GOD after having gone through such deep waters of sorrow. I will be forever grateful for your life, your beautiful spirit, and that simple yet profound hug on a cold winter morning. I love you.

LAURA'S LEGACY OF LOVE

by Kathi

When I think of Laura, I think of the word JOY.
Her positive attitude and outlook permeated the space around her! I am
so grateful that our paths crossed 10 years ago on a cruise ship, of all
places! As Laura said, "It was a 'God thing'!" Laura was my wellness coach,
business mentor, spiritual adviser, and most of all, my friend. I am a better
person for having known Laura. Her life was a blessing to me and to so
many others. She was a role model for living in faith, hope, and love. Her
legacy of love lives on through those of us who knew her.

MY LOVING GRATITUDE
TO LAURA PALMORE

by Karen Roach

I was so blessed to have Laura Palmore as a personal friend in my life for many years.

We met through Shaklee about 30 years ago, and talked on the phone 1-2 times/month, also seeing each other at conventions. She was truly an angel on this earth. She was one of my spiritual mentors, always calling to pray for me and sending me letters of encouragement. When she was ill the last few months of her life, she kept calling me to see how I was doing and to pray for me over the phone. I look forward to the day I reunite with her again in Heaven, and can laugh & play together for eternity. Anyone who knew Laura was blessed.

SWEET LAURA

by Bethany & Pete Christianson

It is really hard to imagine a year has already passed.
I (Bethany) came across some really precious videos recently on my
iPhone. They were taken Christmas 2013. I believe it captures Laura in
her element, singing with her powerful and beautiful voice we all love. I
have no doubt she is praising The Lord with all that is in her now- espe-
cially with her God given voice. I'm really thankful for the reminder of
Laura, to see her beautiful face, to hear her voice as she sings, and to see all
our family together again. We hope this video brings you joy in remem-
bering our dear Laura- her smile, her laugh, her voice, her joy and Hope!
We miss her, and will forever be impacted by her beautiful life.

SOMETIMES PEOPLE COME INTO YOUR LIFE THAT CHANGES EVERYTHING!

by Elena Giacomin Dennis

Laura, you and the Caribous came into my life at such a significant time in my life and business. Your exuberance for God, Yeshua, and the power of the Holy Spirit at work in your life and in this world resonated whenever I spent time with you or heard you talk on our conference calls. You were a wonderful example of love, encouragement and faith. You made me a better woman and I thank you!

SWEET SHAKLEE GRANDMA

by Tiffany Dennis

I remember the first time I met you, Laura! It was at Krystle's Christmas tea a few years ago and as soon as I was introduced you took me in your arms, gave me a hug and said, "I'm your Grandma!"

Boy did I sure feel the grandma type of love flowing from your sweet smile and touch. It's hard to believe that it was just a couple of years ago. Every time I saw you after that you always had the sweetest smile and open arms with kind words of hope and encouragement. I clearly remember the last time I spoke with you. It was the middle of March of last year. You called me up out of the blue because God laid me on your heart to pray for me and with me over the phone. I remember you said something to the effect of "don't give up... God has great things for you! The devil will try to defeat you, but grab a hold of God's promises and stand tall. God will use your story!". I am so thankful that Jesus saw fit to place you in my life, even if for just a short time. How I wish that it would have been longer and I could have grown soo much more spiritually, emotionally, and in my business. I am also thankful that He saw fit to place Krystle in your life and also in mine. She carries on your words of wisdom to me all the time and quotes your life convictions/standards and I swear it is your voice speaking directly to me! Because of your obedience in starting a book of God's promises to you, I have began a book of God's promises to me as well. I know that they will carry me through times of difficulty and I know that "the shadows of the valley of death" will be just that... shadows. Thank you for the impact you have made on my life Laura and the legacy you have left behind through the people who are left here on earth to smile at the memory of you and all that you were! I am blessed to have known you, my sweet Grandma!!!

LAURA PALMORE, MY FOREVER FRIEND

by Kay

Today, my dear friend has been much on my mind in sweet ways.
It was a day of remembering.
Do you know how sometimes our car can be our sanctuary? Allow me
to tell you a story. This morning at Bible study, a friend gifted me with a
wonderful CD of the most beautiful praise music. As I listened to the first
song in my sanctuary (my car), it was as if Laura was right there praising
our Savior with me. It was a song I knew she would love and as I continued
listening to the music, I sensed the CD was a gift from Laura through my
friend on this day marking the anniversary of the Shepherd King coming
to take her hand and walk her home. Then I started meditating on who
Laura was....she was an exhorter and used that gift which God put in her
to full tilt. She was an encourager, most compassionate,and always stopped
for that person God put in front of her. I recall a conversation that our
Caribou group , praying Shaklee friends, had about the legacy we hoped to
leave. Laura said, "I want each person that I pass by to be better because of
my having been there." Laura, my dear sister in Christ, I believe you
fulfilled that legacy and God said, "Well done, my good and faithful
servant."

MY SISTER-FRIEND

by Tonya Patterson

I've been writing this letter in my head every day for the past couple of weeks. Getting it on paper....well, that's a different story. How do you put into words the magnitude of gratitude you feel for someone who created an eternal legacy in your life? How do you begin to express the depth of the friendship, the tears and the laughter, shared heartaches and joys, and just knowing that at any moment if I needed you, you were always there? Even now, a year later, I still pick up my phone at times and start to call you. Your name is still there in my "favorites" list. I suppose it always will be. Oh, how I miss our conversations. There are few friends with which you can say every single conversation was meaningful. With you, my friend, that was always true. There was never a time that we talked (and that was almost daily) that you weren't gushing with gratitude for one thing or another. Every conversation, meaningful...always uplifting and God honoring. And our adventures.....I smile just thinking about them. From Washington D.C. to San Francisco and islands in the Caribbean to every-where in between- we have had the joy of traveling, sight-seeing, exploring and dreaming together in beautiful places across the US and beyond. And exploring together usually involved getting lost. I can't help but laugh at all the times and all the places we managed to get lost. There were lots of detours and unplanned adventures and they are all part of what makes me smile when I think of you and you always managed to turn every single one of them into a spiritual or life lesson. Mostly, I am just so grateful for all of the love and encouragement that you poured into me all of the years of our friendship. Your friendship was such a gift from God to me, and even though you stepped into eternity long before I was ready to give you up, all that your friendship planted in me continues to blossom and grow and make me a better person. The world isn't the same without you, but I am a far better person because of you...and I am forever grateful that God allowed me to be blessed with your friendship for more than a decade. The past year has felt like an eternity at times, but I do have the joy of knowing that one day, we'll be taking long walks and catching up again. Until then, I will be missing you my sister-friend.

TELL LAURA I LOVE HER

by Wally Stewart

My title is from a song that was popular when we were kids, Laura, but it is what I want to shout!

I can't remember if we ever said "I love you" to each other, but I heard you say it with my eyes every time I saw you. I'm seeing the teenager who liked to say "I'm your Momma," as a college freshman (Interesting because I was older than you.) who became the enduring friend and ever hopeful matchmaker, the last time I visited, (at a party.) you pointed to the first woman who came through your door and said (In your excited voice.) "She's single!" (If any of the women you had me meet had been like you not in physical beauty but in the great qualities that made you who you were–I would have gotten excited.) I'm hearing your very distinctive laugh and the joy it put in my heart. I'm hearing your wonderful singing when we were in the Lindsey Wilson College choir and remembering the fun we had in it. (I saw a video on this site of you singing at a Christmas party and did a harmony line. I wish we had gotten around to doing the duet in your church, that we sometimes talked about.)

I loved visiting you and at your Ashbury Lane house, I saw the first of two presents you gave me (With Al's help.) that still fill me with love and such wonderful memories. Jeanie was two weeks old then in her bassinet–Chris hadn't gotten here yet and they still call me "Uncle." Your babies became great adults and I know you were/are very proud of them–I am also.

There are more memories than I have room to put here and they are all about the love, that you so freely gave, to anyone lucky enough to meet you. I think it is not coincidence that Laura, love and lucky all start with the same letter and I was extremely lucky to be Al's roommate when he met you, for I would have missed out on such great joy if I had not been–I'm laughing, remembering that Al introduced me as "my roommate" for several years until you finally said "He's not your roommate, I am! I also remember when you said "Al, all you and Wally talk about is who is getting the most bald and I don't want to hear anymore about it! I'm putting my foot down!" That ended it except for the 40th birthday song I wrote for Al- "Yesterday When I Had Hair." (I can hear Chris and Jeanie saying "Play the hair song" when I visited after that.) These memories are coming to me through a curtain of great sorrow, because I miss you so much and wish you were still physically on this earth, with perfect health and no pain, but the joy of knowing you can't be blocked by that curtain and it fills me again with the love I always felt from and had/have for you. Laura and love are synonymous and I was lucky enough to experience both for a long time. I loved you from first knowing you and will as long as I have breath and memory-lucky, lucky me.

LAURA

by Rocío Del Mar Rodríguez Pulido

(Added on 4/30/2017 - This memorial page allowed my now wife, Rocío, to write a letter to my mom even though they had never met.)

I know that my words may sound strange because although I was not fortunate enough to be able to share time with you, although I do not even speak your language, although I live many miles away, I know that I know you.

I know you through the people you loved when you were here on earth and that you continue to love and protect from the sky.

I know you through the beautiful smile of your daughter Jeannie, the warm embrace she gave me when she met me at the lake house, her kindness when she offered to lend me clothes for the cold, her kind invitation to share with her family The barbecue the night before Easter, I know how you take care of others when I see Jeannie taking care of Steve, her father, and brother.

I know you through your husband, I know your hospitality, which was the same that he gave me to allow him to stay in his house, I know your kindness through him, since every morning he wished me good morning with a beautiful smile and At night he said goodbye with a warm embrace of Chris and beautiful wishes for me, I know your concern for the welfare of others every time Mr. Al was concerned to make me feel at home, I know your generosity through him and His numerous invitations, I know your tenderness when I see Mr. Al talking to Gracie.

And I know you through your Son Chris, I know your infinite ability to give love to your loved ones through him, I know the gratitude that you always had for life and for everything that surrounds you and that inspired your child to start Your wonderful work in your name, I know the patience you had when I see your son being so patient with me, I know how loving you are when I see Chris treating me with so much affection, I know your sweetness when I see the sweetness of Chris, I feel your love when I look at Chris's eyes full of love.

Today I was reading the blog, in which many of your loved ones wrote you and want to write you these short words, because although our paths never crossed, today I feel part of my life through the lives of your loved ones, you did the Best of the works not only with Jeannie, Al, and Chris but with all the people with whom you shared, as someone mentioned in the blog, you sowed many seeds in all, which germinate giving beautiful fruits that will last forever.

That day, I wrote my own letter to her sitting at our favorite lunch place.

MOMMY

by Your Forever Grateful Son, Chris

Mommy,

Where to start... It's been an eventful year since you've been gone.

I've had to really get in touch with living a life where I can't talk with you every day. I miss your voice. I miss the way you would sneeze. You sounded like a little Tweety bird and I miss it. I miss our walks and how you made me feel like the most special person in the entire world.

I'd like to let you know that Dad and I are spending a lot more time together. I moved in with him out in Shelbyville six or so weeks ago and we are now not only father and son but roommates. This arrangement is perfect! Well, almost perfect. We both have a big piece missing from our lives which is you. I know that even if I get to live a long life nothing will ever fill the space that is me missing you.

I think that you would be proud of me. I've internalized the truth that we all have the choice of what we want to focus on. I daily think of you and when I get sad in these moments I make a choice of how long I want to be in that moment. I think of what you would want and if it's a sad moment I redirect. I'm having to stay in this place a little longer right now to write this.

Right now, I'm at our sushi restaurant, Kansai. I'm having a Derby Roll in your honor. I wish you were here to share this moment with me. I remember the last time I was here before you passed. I brought a Derby Roll home for you. You couldn't eat it because of the medication. I ended up eating it.

You sure did leave some big shoes to fill. I've been doing my best to shine the light of gratitude that you have left in me on the world. I foresee millions of people sharing gratitude throughout the entire world because of your love. There is a huge wave of gratitude coming; it's going to wipe some of the negativity and hate out of the world. This will be happening because you chose to love me. I love you so much, Mom.

Your Forever Grateful Son, Chris

This was a very powerful way to celebrate my mom and her passing. I felt I had created something that was unique. This was an amazing expression of gratitude for all of these people, to take the time and write a letter to someone who wasn't alive and allow it to be shared online. Powerful things can happen when people share love and allow it to be shared with the world. These people are pioneers with big hearts and open minds.

Many years have passed since this special day. It was one year to the day later that I discovered the simplest way to achieve what was at the core of my original idea.

If we love someone, we will be sad if we outlive them. This is the flip side to all of the good memories, feelings, and experiences with another person. With love there will always be loss. We can take the good memories and be grateful for having them, for having the time and the experience of loving another person. The amazing thing about love is that it can go on. If someone you know dies, you can continue to love them.

I continue to love my mom when I think of her and her love for me. How she believed in and always cared for me. The hard thing is getting past the trauma of the death. Everyone's time is different. Death and things surrounding it are like a hurricane. At the moment of loss we are in the eye of the storm. As time passes we find some distance from the eye.

This tremendous pain only exists because of the love we were giving. Love is a gift, and the more we appreciate it the more it will grow. Wouldn't our loved ones want us to remember them the way they were...listening, caring, laughing? We can remember the time we had with them and be grateful for it.

DEAR SHIKHA

by Janhvi Parmar

November 2020 will mark your second death anniversary. I feel a void even today. However, I have learned to live with it. The first couple of months were extremely painful; I had lost the will to do anything. Hunger had left my side, too. Enjoyment felt like a guilt trip, as if I were making fun of you not being here with me.

Every person has a go-to human, a person you can count on for always being there no matter what, a person who selflessly sets out to be your problem solver, who motivates you on your bad day, who gives you their arms to drown in your sorrows, who believes in you when no one does, who understands your emotions whether good or bad. When you left me for your heavenly abode, I felt so alone. It felt as if my life support ceased to function. Not being able to meet you, see you, and hug you felt like a burden on my shoulders that kept getting heavier by every passing day. You were my little baby sister but scolded me and got me to do the right thing whenever I strayed away.

Coping with your death has by far been the hardest barrier that I have had to overcome. I spent most of my days alone reading books on how to overcome death. Then, one fine day I stumbled upon one of my old favorites, The Laws of the Spirit World by Korshed Bhavnagri. Reading it for the second time gave me further perspective on the truths of life, saving me from drowning in my thoughts and exposing clarity and understanding.

As per my understanding, Earth is our school where we learn, gain experiences and try to purify our souls to reach a higher level. There are seven levels, or realms, or planes, in the spirit world (where you are right now, our soul's real home). We come here on earth for a short time to complete our training and schooling and then return to our real home.

According to the abovementioned author, "We take rebirth to go higher, and most people on Earth go down because of the widespread evil influence in your world. Many good souls over here have to think hundreds of times before taking rebirth in your world, as no one likes to go down, except the real evil souls – the devils. Many good souls are reborn in your world to do good, to fight evil and to spread harmony and goodness, but unfortunately, the evil influence is so strong that their subconscious minds request God Almighty to bring them back home immediately. They hate to go down to the lower Realms and their subconscious minds do not allow them to do wrong – extreme wrong – so they don't understand where to turn in a world so influenced by evil. That is why good souls are unhappy and miserable. So, without their conscious knowledge, their subconscious minds appeal to God Almighty to bring them back to their spiritual home. This is the reason people on Earth have the saying. 'Those who die young are God's favorites.'

You were God's favorite , Shikha, and he could not see you suffer in pain. Hence, he called you back to heal you and free you from your physical suffering. I have not stopped missing you, Shikha. The emptiness that your absence has left behind has now been filled with immense gratitude. You were not only my baby sister, but you were also my guiding star. You always paved ways for me when you were alive. Your passing woke my soul to have a deeper knowledge about life after death and knowing that there is so much more I still have to learn and explore to respect my calling for this newfound spiritual life. Thank you for being the "zariya" (meaning "the way") for my calling. Ever so grateful to you in this lifetime, all our previous lifetimes, and all the lifetimes that are yet to come.

Lovingly Yours,
Janhvi

G-DAD

by Aeon Solo

Hey G-Dad, it's been a while. Ten years, is it? I wouldn't know by now. I can't remember much before then. Losing you was the catalyst to most of my problems; I was just a boy. And when I saw you in that bed, it broke my heart. But Mum's more so. Losing you destroyed her. Even now, I hear her cry sometimes. I hate it when she drinks. She used to always get upset about you and feel as though the world was against her. She'd say losing a parent feels like losing half of yourself. I dread losing her and Dad. I should have said no that day, because now I can't even see you when you are alive in my mind; all I see is an empty shell of biology. I saw the difference between life and death. What I saw wasn't you anymore, but it's singed into my brain, and I can't get it out. It overrules everything, every memory of you.

I should think about you more often. You and I both know the cliché 'I think about you every day' is utter bollocks. We have a new picture of you in the living room now, so I can see you again. The real you, not just crude flesh. Sometimes we chat about how I used to sneak the TV remote from you when you were sleeping, and how you tutted throughout the entire Lord of The Rings. You'd hate it today, though, no horse racing, no sports, no pubs. I'd like to believe you were like me and saw the bullshit for what it was. Most people gobbled up the narrative. The future is looking bleak right about now. Everyone is walking around in masks wherever you go; I'm one of the only ones who's not; it's madness. But I'm the mad one, apparently. I'd like to think you would stand at my side if you were here.

Writing this got me thinking of you, and towards the end. I remember briefly the day you went to the nursing home. You begged Mum and Dad not to let them take you because you knew you wouldn't come back, and I, being an oblivious kid, didn't fight for you. I know you had cancer, and that Mum and Dad couldn't care for you anymore. If it were up to me, I wouldn't let you go to that place. As devastating as it would be, if you wanted to die with us, so be it. Instead you were alone. And in that awful place... it may as well have been death's waiting room. I'll try my best not to let Mum and Dad suffer this same fate.

Losing you was tough for Dad; it was like losing a real father for him. You knew his father was...unsavoury, to say the least, but you were good enough to fill the void for him. He must have liked you; he was your taxi driver after all. When I ask him to take me to the gym once, he has a hissy fit. And you supported him when he went "working away." He was so worried you'd think less of him, and that you'd want Mum to leave him because of one unlucky night. But you supported him when his family didn't. He'll be forever grateful. When you asked for him toward the end, he was so honoured... because you are his real father at heart.

I'm sorry I haven't visited your grave in God knows how long, but it's too much for me. If you're watching me now, you'd be thinking I'm a soft sod, crying me bloody eyes out writing this. Did we give you hope after Mary died? Did life become worth living again when you lived with us? I know we kids were probably annoying, but a good annoying, I hope. And Lord of The Rings is great, by the way! That's my Star Wars before Star Wars. TV Gold is crap! I still have One Foot in the Grave theme stuck in my head, and what's the other one...New Tricks? That one became palatable after a while. More of a... I was forced to like it I guess, like Stockholm syndrome. I'm watching an episode of One Foot in the Grave while writing now. Dare I say it's not too bad? Ha!

Anyway, I hope I do you proud. If ghosts are real and you are knocking about the place, you better not be watching me. I saw someone one night in my room who I first thought was Dad. Mum said it could have been you. I don't know about the ghost thing. I'm open to it, but it's a tough one to commit to at the moment. If it was you, you scared the bejesus out of me. I couldn't step foot in my own bedroom alone for two weeks after that night.

You were a good man by anyone's standards. They made a darts cup in your honour round our parts, which you might like the sound of. A friend of mine actually won the trophy one year and donated it to us. So, I am proud to say you are my grandfather. I just hope I can live up to you. Dad too.

Goodbye, but I'll always keep you in my heart.

DEAR MOM & DAD

by Barbara Faison

As I reflect on my life and think about the way you worked together to do so many things including buy a new home and make sure my brother and I went to (and graduated from) college, I am so grateful for having you as parents.

Growing up as the child of a teacher and a librarian has given me a rich love for words. Reading and writing came natural to me and I was encouraged to express myself. Thank you for this honor. Your loving support of my creative spirit and musings has allowed me to develop a strong sense of self and self-acceptance.

You both instilled in me the importance of having discipline and being committed to my goals. I know your encouragement is what gave me the courage and permission to write my book, *Why Struggle? life is too short to wear tight shoes*. I still smile thinking about seeing you both with the book in your hands. Thank you for believing in me.

I am grateful I was able to express my reverence and love for you both before you left to be together in the next life. I feel so blessed to have been your child. I am forever in love with you both! Thank you for being my parents.

Your daughter,
Barbara

DEAR MOM

by Marc Levine

Dear Mom,

Thank you for being here on planet earth. Thank you for being my mom for 24 years. You had an enormous impact in a short time. You showed me what unconditional love looks like. In a world where not every child knows love, my sister and I never had to wonder. We always knew that we had your love and your support. You supported my love of sports as well as my love of sports writing, and gave me space to explore.

Thank you for being there through thick and thin. Thank you for letting me know I was okay when things didn't feel okay.

Thank you for passing down your kindness and humor. I use my humor every day and always for good.

I love you very much and imagine you're having fun wherever you are and in whatever form.

Love,
Marc

HOW COULD YOU HAVE EVER KNOWN?

A LETTER OF GRATITUDE

by Bobby Kountz

Bobby Kountz is an inspirationalist and the author of The Someday Solution.

Dear Denae,

How could you have ever known the power of an email?

~ OR DID YOU?

How could you have ever known how much I needed my brother, your husband, and all the rest of the family?

~ OR DID YOU?

How could you have ever known that both he and they might just need me too?

~ OR DID YOU?

We constantly hear that God works in mysterious ways; He seeks out those who offer up in prayer "big challenges" and then effortlessly places solutions in their hearts. His solution for your prayer was simple yet profound. Most things that come from God are... I remember like it was just yesterday receiving that email..., your gift that just showed up one day in my in-box.

How did you know what to say? How did you know the right words to use that would stir my heart and soul into action and give me the courage to reply back? And then I remembered, God has full command of all resources, both words and angels! He chose an angel (you) to re-unite a family in the glory of love. How could you have possibly known that the strength of this love could melt away years of emptiness?

~ OR DID YOU?

My Dear Denae, this letter of gratitude is a testament to your life, your love, your legacy, and the profound difference you made in mine. I am just one of so many... They say it's impossible for a heart to physically grow in size, and that may be true. What cannot be denied though is how one loving, caring, thoughtful, human being can impact the life of another. Your words and actions were the catalyst for my heart to grow in capacity. How could you have ever known that your words would help my heart grow three times its normal size with just an email?

~ OR DID YOU?

There is no doubt in my mind, or in my heart, that you knew exactly what you were doing. You knew exactly what to say. The words were given to you from above and delivered into my heart through you and your love for your husband and your family that you so graciously decided to "share" with me, with us, actually. How could you have known that you would have an almost instant connection with my beautiful wife?

~ OR DID YOU?

Could you see into the very fiber of her soul and know just how good she would be for everybody else too? Of course you did, because it was revealed to you, and as the angel you were and still are, you answered the call from above and heeded the words that were placed into your heart and re-united a family. You have given me, us, all of us the greatest gift ever, "love"! For that, I am eternally thankful. For that, I am eternally grateful. How could you have ever known that, together, we would find a way to celebrate and honor you through our love?

~OR DID YOU?

Of course you did! So, as you look down now upon us my loving guardian angel, I ask that you deliver that same message of love into the heart of your husband, so that, over time, he can understand that you, although departed from this earthly realm and your earthly body, will always be with us in all that you did, all whom you loved, and all that you were and now are in heaven for all eternity.

Know that you are alive and well in my heart, forever. Also, know that I will always love you. I will honor your gift of love, not just with words, but with my actions. I commit today irrevocably in front of all of you and in the presence of God to demonstrate through my actions, my love, your gift, Denae, to my family, and all of the rest of humanity.

How could you have ever known? Now we know: God works through angels.

Fly free, Denae; fly free! I love you. We all love you. Thank you! Thank you for the gift of you, your grace, your spirit, and most of all, your gift.

Fly free, Denae; fly free!

ROSAURA

by JessMag

Rosaura Barbarita fue el nombre de mi abuelita materna, ella lastimosamente falleció en el año 2012, y aunque siempre le demostré lo mucho que la quería y lo importante que era en mi vida, hoy quiero escribirle la siguiente carta:

Abuelita, a pesar de que han pasado muchos años de tu partida al cielo (porque estoy segura que estás en el cielo) quiero decirte que siempre recuerdo lo mucho que me mimabas y todos los cuidados que tenías conmigo, tengo intactos los recuerdos de cuando era niña y de las vacaciones que pasaba en tu casa, tu sonrisa y la forma en como dormías a mi lado son mis recuerdos favoritos.

Como tu vivías en una ciudad diferente a la mía, cuando sabía que nos ibas a visitar, contaba los días para tenerte a mi lado. Tú no lo sabías, pero las charlas que teníamos para ponernos al día de todo, era lo mejor para mí, me encantaba preguntarte por todos mis tíos, mis primos, todo lo que te había sucedido mientras no estábamos juntas, me encantaba escuchar de ti cada detalle, realmente es algo que extraño mucho, y obviamente, cuando regresabas a tu casa, era un momento muy triste para mí, cada despedida era un mar de lágrimas de ambas.

Si pudiera pedir un deseo, sin duda pediría volverte a ver para darte un abrazo muy fuerte, aprovecharía para decirte cuanto te extraño y todo lo que ha pasado en mi vida desde tu ausencia, sería breve, pero te contaría lo mejor, para que te sientas feliz y tranquila allá donde estás. Aunque estoy segura, que desde donde estás, nos cuidas, en especial a mi mamá y a mis hermanos; yo considero que tú eres mi ángel de la guarda que siempre me acompaña, y que me ha cuidado, incluso cuando he estado en serio peligro.

Abuelita (así te decía siempre), quiero que sepas, que siempre te llevo en mi corazón, cuando hablo de ti, te recuerdo con mucho cariño dibujando una sonrisa en mi rostro; dicen que las abuelitas sostienen nuestras manos por instantes, pero nuestro corazón lo sostienen para siempre, y confirmo que es así, ya que tu sostienes mi corazón y por siempre vivirás en él, nunca nadie ocupará ni reemplazará el lugar tan especial que ocupas en mi vida entera.

JessMag

Rosaura Barbarita was the name of my maternal grandmother. She sadly passed away in 2012, and although I always showed her how much I loved her and how important she was in my life, today I want to write her the following letter:

Grandma,

Despite the fact that many years have passed since your departure to heaven (because I'm sure you are in heaven), I want to tell you that I always remember how much you cared for and pampered me. I have held onto the memories of when I was a girl, the vacations I spent at your house, your smile, and the way you slept next to me. These are my favorite memories.

Because you lived in a different city than me, when I knew you were coming to visit, I'd always count the days until I would be by your side. You didn't know it, but our talks and catching up on all things was so special to me. I loved asking you about all my uncles, cousins, and everything that had happened to you while we were apart. I loved hearing every little detail and I really miss this a lot. Obviously, when you returned home, it was a very sad moment for me. Each goodbye was a sea of tears from both of us.

If I could make a wish, without a doubt, I would ask to see you again. I'd give you a very strong hug and take the opportunity to tell you how much I missed you and everything that has happened in my life since your absence. It would be brief, but I would tell you all the good things so that you would be happy and calm wherever you are. Although I am sure that wherever you are, you are taking care of us, especially my mother and my brothers. I consider you to be my guardian angel who always accompanies me, and who has taken care of me, especially when I have been in serious danger.

Grandma (that's what I always called you), I want you to know that I always carry you in my heart; when I talk about you, I remember you fondly drawing a smile on my face. They say that grannies hold our hands for moments, but our hearts, they hold it forever, and I confirm that it is so, since you hold my heart and you will live in it forever; no one will ever occupy or replace the special place you occupy in my entire life.

JessMag

ABUELO

by Viko

A mi abuelo...

Si pienso en ti, sólo sonrío, el alma se me estremece y las lágrimas se escapan, es tan grande el vacío que dejaste como grande fue tu existencia, ya son 18 años tal vez más y aún estás presente en mí vida, cada día, con tu ternura, tu alma de niño, tu gran corazón y sobre todo tu sabiduría, eres de esas personas que solo creces viendo y quieres emular. Te recuerdo siempre sentado en tu sillón mirando por la ventana el huerto que construiste en un lote baldío frente a la casa, y sabes eso eras, vida entre las sombras y aunque ese huerto ya no está como muchas cosas buenas que se fueron contigo, quedó lo más importante y que representa el fin de tu existencia, un legado que el tiempo no ha podido borrar y sé que no lo hará, porque hoy te veo en tantas personas, veo tu honestidad, tu rectitud, tu deseo de superación y así muchos no te conocieran o tal vez no te recuerden, lo mejor de ti va a permanecer en ellos.

Jamás existirán suficientes palabras para expresar lo agradecida y bendecida que me siento de ser parte de esta familia, una familia que junto a mi abuela con tanto esfuerzo, sacrificio y amor construyeron. Ojalá te pudiera abrazar y sentarme contigo a la mesa y que me pellizcaras la mano como siempre lo hacías, sé que ya no puedo, pero también sé que estás aquí y nos cuidas a todos, nos proteges, nos guías y quiero que sepas que tu ejemplo, tus enseñanzas viven conmigo, y que te agradeceré siempre que lo mejor de mi vida lo tengo gracias a ti.

Te extraño y te mando un abrazo de mi alma a tu alma...

To my grandfather...

If I think of you, I just smile, my soul shudders, and tears escape. The emptiness that you left is great, and how great was your existence. It has already been eighteen years or maybe more and you are still present in my life, every day. With your tenderness, your child's soul, your big heart, and, above all, your wisdom. You were one of the people that I wanted to be like when I grew up. I always remember you sitting in your armchair looking out the window at the garden that you built on the vacant lot in front of the house. I knew that you were always casting light into the shadows, and although the garden no longer exists, many good things that you left do. I remain the most important thing that represents the end of your existence, a legacy that time has not been able to erase and I know that it will not, because today I see you in so many people. I see your honesty, your rectitude, your desire to improve, and so many other things. Maybe they did not know you or do not remember you, but the best of you will remain in them. There will never be enough words to express how grateful and blessed I feel to be part of this family, a family that together with my grandmother who worked and sacrificed for love they built. I wish I could hug you and sit with you at the table and that you would pinch my hand as you always did. I know you can't any longer, but I also know that you are here, take care of us all, protect us, guide us. I want you to know that your teachings, for example, live with me, and that I will always be thankful for this wonderful life that is all thanks to you. I miss you and send you a hug from my soul to your soul...

Viko

WHAT IS A GRANDMOTHER?

by Parker McGuffey

Contrary to most children's families, there once was a boy born into a family with only one set of grandparents. However, this is not a farce or a tale of neglect; this is a story of the love given to a boy equaling that of two grandparents. This extraordinary woman was this boy's world when he was around her. As you may have assumed, this woman I am talking so fondly of is my one and only grandmother.

Grandma, as I have grown into the eighteen-year-old body I have now, I realize just how lucky I am to have such an amazing woman in my life. Most times kids' grandparents are not prevalent in their lives or make an impact on them. Grandma, I want to give you a gift; I want to show you how I view a grandmother purely from having and loving you all of my life.

A grandmother is a child's world. She lets you watch cartoons for hours when your parents let you watch Animal Planet and play on a calculator. When you're small, you sleep in her bed with her, nagging her about wanting to play with the heated comforter the whole time, and finally fall asleep after you make her sing the lullabies Mom and Pop usually sing you until she gets them right. A grandma is someone who, once she gets them right, remembers them the rest of the endless sleepovers in the future.

However, I will warn against ever allowing grandmothers near your head if they lure you in with, "Here sweetie, let me comb/dry your hair." (Allow three days for recovery; gently massage your head with shampoo in a salt bath twice daily.)

A grandmother is someone who can yell at you but make you feel how much she loves you at the same time. She can hear the worst thing about you and defend you until the end of the earth.

She will listen to a seven-year-old's babbly nonsense while sitting on the edge of the bed looking through photo albums when I still had jaundice. (She also teaches you fun nurse terms like that.)

This reflection is not to talk about everything we did together because that is not how my grandmother is. It is to show the character of a selfless, loving, mature woman who will spend the rest of her life listening to a three-year-old's gibberish and just hold a conversation of nonsense.

Grandma, all of those times that I woke up next to you as a kid in the morning I think would be the best way to explain how much I love you. We would wake up to your alarm clock. I was always on your left. You would start doing physical therapy. I would sometimes do it with you just because I thought it was fun or I would sit there cross-legged and count along with you. We would sneak past Grandpa's room and you would pour me a bowl of cereal then go and 'get ready.' But I never thought you needed to get ready.

I see you as the most beautiful woman in the world, and I am a terrible person to ask how your hair looks because I will always have the same reply. It's perfect. Don't ask me if I love you because I don't think words express how much you mean to me. As I have matured, I have deepened my understanding as to why you are wonderful. At age five, you could ask me why I love my grandma and I would say because she is my grandma. Now I don't even think I could name all of the reasons. You are the only person I will walk more slowly for. Just because I love when you hold my arm. You are the only person I let kiss my cheek with lipstick on. You have never missed spending a birthday with me.

If I know one thing for certain, it is that I will love my grandmother and never stop. You hold a special place in my heart and I wish there was a way to express emotions through words. If you just glean one thing from this letter, know that I would go to the end of the world for you, if that was what you asked. I may be a grandma's boy... I don't know.

When I was thinking of what to write, I decided to find out what the true meaning of a grandmother is.

What is a grandmother?

A grandmother is a remarkable woman.

She is a perfect combination of kindness, laughter, and love.

She overlooks our faults, encourages our dreams, and praises our every success.

ABUELITO

by Lina Isabel

Abuelito,

Hace 4 años ya de tu partida y aun te extraño como el primer día, extraño tus enseñanzas, tu compañía, tus dichos y refranes, tu sonrisa y sobre todo tu protección. Te adelantaste bastante en tu partida, no pudiste conocer a Juan Martín, no sabes cómo anhele que mi hijo creciera a tu lado, aprendiendo los cuentos que te sabias y que tan jocosamente contabas, como el del zorro y el conejo o el baile de los animales, haberle enseñado las capitales y cuanto vivían los animales, como lo hiciste conmigo, jugar y reír como sé que lo hubieran hecho, siempre le hablo a él de ti, el conoce al abuelito Carlos y yo espero que se parezca a ti, que podías hacer de todo y lo que no sabías lo buscabas en libros y aprendías constantemente.

Aún recuerdo cuando te veía tejer tus atarrayas, o arreglar los electrodomésticos o lo que se dañara en la casa, te observaba con esa paciencia y dedicación con la que hacías todo, cantabas y te reías y me contabas las historias que te llenaban de alegría cuando ibas a pescar, o cuando habías viajado a cierto lugar, porque conociste muchos lugares que te hicieron un hombre sabio, me decías que habías crecido en el campo y que sabias ordeñar vacas y arriar ganado, recuerdo que podías pasar horas contando esas historias, que ahora recuerdo con tanta nostalgia de saber que no las volveré a escuchar.

Me decías que quería verme graduada, pero antes de fallecer me dijiste que ya no alcanzabas, como si supieras que Dios ya te estaba llamando para estar con él, aun así abuelito me gradué, cumplí con lo que tanto anhelabas que era verme ser una profesional y aunque no pudiste acompañarme físicamente sé que desde el cielo estuviste conmigo porque lo sentí y supe que estabas muy orgulloso de mi.

Siempre me decías que estudiara que era lo único que me quedaría, y si abuelito acá estoy volviendo a estudiar, acabo de empezar una especialización y sé que si estuvieras vivo estarías siempre apoyándome y diciéndome que lo haga que estudie que tengo que seguir aprendiendo, o que lea porque siempre eso me enseñaste, recuerdo y digo con mucho orgullo que tú aunque solo estudiaste hasta el grado tercero sabías mil cosas porque leías mucho y hago referencia a que te habías leído un diccionario y cuando yo no sabía el significado de algo te preguntaba por qué siempre tenías la respuesta.

Jugábamos ajedrez y te reías de mi porque no te podía ganar y me molestaba, me decías "tiene que mover las fichas siempre pensando cual voy a mover yo", yo como era mala perdedora te decía que no jugaba más y te ibas a donde la señora que vendía fruta y me traías sandia o una ensalada para contentarme. Recuerdo cuando usabas combinaciones de ropa que para nada salían, solo para que yo te dijera que no combinaban y escogiera tu ropa, me pedías que te cortara las uñas o te arreglara las cejas y a veces me molestaba hacerlo porque prefería hacer otras cosas, ahora no sabes cómo anhelaría poder hacer todo eso, porque cada día desde el 18 de agosto del 2016 te extraño infinitamente.

Hoy a mis 28 años te doy gracias abuelito, por haber compartido conmigo tu vida, por haberme enseñado tanto y por ser mi referente de orgullo y sobre todo por haber dejado en mí una marca tan grande, no solo de amor y enseñanzas, si no de nobleza y tranquilidad, te adoro abuelito y siempre vivirás en mis pensamientos y en mi corazón.

Lina Isabel

Grandpa,

It's been four years since your departure and I still miss you like the first day. I miss your teachings, your company, your sayings, your smile, and, above all, your protection. You were quite old when you departed; you could not meet your grandson, Juan Martin. You do not know how I longed for my son to grow up with you, learning the stories that you knew and that you told so jokingly, such as the fox and the rabbit or the dance of the animals, showing him the capitals and how many animals lived as you did with me, playing and laughing as I know you would have. I always talk to him about you; he knows.

Grandpa Carlos and I hope he looks like you. Oh, how you could do everything and what you did not know you looked for in books and you learned constantly.

I still remember when I saw you weave your cast nets, or fix the appliances or whatever was damaged in the house. I watched you with that patience and dedication with which you did everything. You sang and laughed and told me the stories that filled you with joy, about when you would go fishing, or when you had traveled to a certain place... because you knew many places that made you a wise man; you told me that you had grown up in the field and that you knew how to milk cows and herd cattle. I remember that you could spend hours telling these stories, stories which I now remember with such nostalgia, knowing that I will never hear them again.

You told me that you wanted to see me graduate, but before you passed away you told me that you wouldn't, as if you knew that God was already calling you to be with him; even so, Grandpa, I graduated. I fulfilled what you saw in me and became a professional. And although you could not accompany me physically, I know that you were with me from heaven because I felt it and I knew that you were very proud of me. You always told me to study. If you were here, Grandfather, I'd want to let you know that I am going back to school. I have just started a specialization and I know that if you were alive you would always be supporting me and telling me to continue studying and learning, or to read because you always taught me that. I remember and say with great pride that you, although you only studied up to the third grade, knew thousands of things because you read a lot and I refer to the fact that you had studied the dictionary. Whenever I did not know the meaning of something, I asked you and you always had the answer.

We played chess and you laughed at me because I couldn't beat you and it bothered me. You told me that you have to move the chips, always thinking which one I'm going to move. Since I was a bad loser, I told you that I didn't play anymore and you went to the local lady who sold fruit and brought me watermelon or a salad to please me.

I remember when you used combinations of clothes that did not match at all. I told you that they did not match and I would choose your clothes. You would asked me to cut your nails or fix your eyebrows and sometimes it would bother me to do it because I preferred to do other things. Now you know how I wish I could do all that because every day since August 18, 2016, I miss you infinitely.

Today at 28 years of age, I am grateful for you, Grandfather, for having shared your life with me, for having taught me so much, for being my point of pride, and, above all, for leaving such a great mark on me, not only for your love and teachings, but also for your nobility and tranquility. I adore you, Grandfather, and you will always live in my thoughts and in my heart.

Lina Isabel

MIS ÁNGELES

by Rocío del Mar

Cuando estaba escogiendo el tema sobre el cual escribir sabía que una carta a una persona fallecida iba a ser uno de ellos porque muchas veces tenemos qué expresar por escrito a las personas que ya no están con nosotros, lo que no dijimos cuando los tuvimos cerca.

Hoy quiero hacer un corto homenaje a 3 de las personas que más he amado y que hoy sé que están conmigo cuidándome y protegiéndome desde el cielo:

Abuelito, desde que tengo uso de razón siempre recuerdo que estuviste a mi lado, mis primeros recuerdos de la infancia son junto a ti, recuerdo como a lo lejos reconocía tu carro y como salía corriendo a recibirte por toda la calle hasta que nos encontrábamos, también recuerdo cuando me llevabas al supermercado y hacíamos las compras, aunque las mías eran todas las golosinas que quería comer; de igual manera recuerdo que cada vez que hacía una pataleta, me encerraba en tu habitación y repetía una y otra vez "quiero a mi abuelito, quiero a mi abuelito", porque eras el único que lograba calmarme.

Recuerdo tus lecciones para jugar ajedrez y también cómo nos divertíamos armando los rompecabezas y todos los juegos que compartíamos, recuerdo tus enojos cuando yo ayudaba a las hormigas a que se comieran tus plantas, aunque sé que en el fondo te divertías viéndome defender a esas pequeñas nuevas amigas.

Con el tiempo fui creciendo y te aprendí a conocer mejor, recuerdo todas tus enseñanzas, tus historias, tus anécdotas de todo lo que viviste durante tantos años y que querías que yo conociera.

Agradezco que me enseñarás a amar la música tradicional de mi país y que cultivaras en mi esa pasión por viajar, el entusiasmo con el que me contabas cada uno de tus viajes, cada persona que conocías a través de ellos, hicieron que yo quisiera descubrir ese mundo como tú lo habías hecho; Agradezco que me enseñarás que tengo que luchar y luchar por lo que deseo, que el primer obstáculo no me puede vencer y que simplemente ante cada tropiezo debo levantarme y sobreponerme para vencerlo.

Estuviste conmigo 36 años de mi vida y viviste 93 maravillosos años de la tuya y solo me queda por dar gracias por ser el mejor abuelito que he podido tener, gracias por hacer que cada vez qué te recuerde se dibuje en mis labios una hermosa sonrisa.

Abuelita hace más de 20 años que no estás con nosotros presente y llevo esos mismos 20 años recordándote con tanto amor, siempre te recuerdo como una mujer de carácter fuerte, con voz de mando, dirigiendo su casa y su familia, eres un ejemplo digno de toda una matrona, nunca conocí a alguien que te llevara la contraria o que fuera capaz de decirte no, todos te obedecíamos fielmente y estoy segura que esa fuerza de carácter fue heredada por mi mamá y a su vez ella me lo heredó a mi.

Siempre voy a recordar la forma en que celebrábamos tu cumple-años, siempre era un gran acontecimiento y el más importante para ti, eso con seguridad sí se que lo heredé de ti; pero más allá de las fiestas que tanto te gustaban hacer, era esa pasión por celebrar la vida lo que tanto admiraba de ti.

Gracias abuelita por enseñarme que las mujeres y los hombres somos iguales, algo que para la época en la que tú creciste no era nada fácil.

Tía Yeyi, siempre fuiste una mujer tan amorosa y dulce, tan entregada y pendiente de tu familia, recuerdo como gran parte de los mejores recuerdos de mi infancia los viví a tu lado y por lo mismo hoy te doy gracias por tantos años de amor, por tantos maravillosos recuerdos, por tener siempre un alma joven, gracias por tus historias, por estar siempre feliz, por acompañarme en cada uno de los juegos, por seguirme la idea en cada locura, gracias por tantos cuidados y por tu protección, gracias por siempre verme como una niña pequeña sin importar mi edad.

A los tres solo me resta por darles las gracias por tantas enseñanzas, paciencia y amor, porque hoy soy la mujer que soy en gran parte por ustedes, estoy tan agradecida por ser parte de su familia y porque se que desde el cielo los tres me siguen cuidando y protegiendo, los amo con todo mi corazón.

Rocío del Mar

When I was choosing the topic to write about, I knew that a letter to a deceased person was going to be one of them. Many times in life we don't express our feelings to loved ones and I choose now to do this. Today I want to make a tribute to three of the people that I have loved the most and that today I know are with me, taking care of me and protecting me from heaven.

Grandpa, since I can remember, you were always by my side; my first childhood memories are with you. I remember how in the distance I recognized your car and how I ran to meet you across the street until we met. I also remember when you would take me to the supermarket to buy me things, although mine were all the sweets I wanted to eat; in the same way, I remember that every time I had a tantrum, I would lock myself in your room and repeat over and over again, "I love my grandfather! I want my grandfather!" because you were the only one who managed to calm me down.

I remember the day you took me by the hand and took me to the bank. I had a piggy bank with many, many, many coins and you gave me the money necessary to have my first bank account. I remember you teaching me to play chess, how we had fun putting together the puzzles, and all the games we shared. I remember your anger when I helped the ants to eat your plants, although I know that deep down you had fun watching me defend those little new friends. Over time I grew up and I learned to know you better. I know that you wanted me to learn from all your teachings, your stories, and your experiences from the long life that you lived.

I am grateful that you taught me to love the traditional music of my country and that you cultivated in me the passion for traveling. I also loved the enthusiasm with which you told me about each of your trips and each person you met through them; this made me want to discover that world that you had talked about. I am grateful that you taught me that I have to be strong and fight for what I want, that the first obstacle cannot overcome me and that simply after each stumble I must get up and keep moving forward. You were with me for 36 years of my life and lived 93 wonderful years of yours. I want to give you thanks for being the best grandfather I could have ever had. Thank you for making a beautiful smile appear on my lips every time I remember you.

Grandma has not been with us for more than twenty years, and I have been remembering her with so much love for those same twenty years. I remember her as a woman with a strong character and a commanding voice while directing her house and her family. She was a worthy example of a full matron. I never met anyone that felt differently about you or was capable of saying no to you. We obeyed faithfully and I am sure that this strength of character was inherited by my mother and in turn by me.

I will always remember the way we celebrated your birthday. It was always a great event and the most important to you; that for sure I do know I inherited from you. Beyond the parties that you liked to do so much, it was that passion for celebrating life that I admired so much about you. Thank you granny for teaching me that women and men are equal even though it wasn't that way when you were growing up.

Aunt Yeyi, you were always such a loving and sweet woman, so dedicated and aware of your family. I remember how many of the best memories of my childhood were lived by your side, and, for the same reason, today I thank you for so many years of love, for so many wonderful memories, for always having a young soul. Thank you for your stories, for always being happy, for accompanying me in each of the games, for following my ideas in very crazy things. Thank you so much for your care and your protection. Thank you for always seeing me as a little girl, regardless of my age.

All three of you remain with me and I thank you for so many lessons, patience and love. Today I am the woman that I am in large part because of you. I am so grateful for being part of your family and I know that from heaven you continue to care and protect me. I love you with all my heart.

Rocío del Mar

CONNECTIONS

"Happiness is a simple game of lost and found: Lose the things you take for granted, and you will feel great happiness once they are found."
  Richelle E. Goodrich

I have had a few memorable gratitude connections. These generally happen when someone shares something they are grateful for which I cannot and will not experience because circumstances don't allow it.

My gratitude connection with Fred was one of these. I was on the Punching Depression Tour. After three big city stops, I decided to take the tour to Las Vegas. I was with Sister Loosy, the best gratitude wing nun in the business, and we were traveling through Vegas, stopping at various crowded places. I met Fred at one of these stops and asked him what he was grateful for. Fred shared that he was grateful for his biological mom for having put him up for adoption. He understood that this was a tough choice, but that it was the best one for both of them. He could look at his life, where he was, the family that ended up adopting him, and express his gratitude. To this day, this is still one of the most honest and beautiful gratitudes shared with me.

The amazing thing about gratitude is that when we hear what others are grateful for, we reflect more deeply on various aspects of our own lives. Now, I wasn't adopted; I had a wonderful mom who cared for me all her life. This is something I'd taken for granted. Fred shared something so true and so piercing that it gave me the opportunity to be grateful for this aspect of my life and appreciate growing up with my biological parents.

All these letters, interviews, and videos are instruments to shine the mirror of gratitude back at the viewer and make a gratitude connection happen, a magical connection that allows an ordinary day to become extraordinary through the power of gratitude.

I once visited Cincinnati and really liked it. I started going there often, sometimes two to three days at a time. I found an amazing

AirBNB downtown near an awesome coffee shop. It was only a couch to sleep on, but it was nice and had free parking. This was a luxury one-bedroom condo and the guy only charged $20 a night. Downtown, the parking alone for a day was $15.

I knew that the city had a lot to offer, and it was far enough away from home that it felt like a mini retreat and adventure. The great thing was that I could walk around downtown and meet people. The coffee shop was fantastic. I loved working on the website and meeting people in the coffee shop. I especially loved the bottomless cup. I'm grateful for bottomless cups.

I was walking around downtown and came across a homeless man named Rick. I was smoking cigarettes at this time in my life, and he asked me for one. I gave him one and we started talking. It was freezing out, but this guy wasn't complaining to me. He wanted some money for food, or so he said. Normally, in this situation, I just go buy the person some food. I went into the nearby restaurant and ordered him some food. I came back out and talked to him while we waited for the food.

I recounted how my mom had died and how I had started a website on which I was posting captured moments of gratitude, big or small.

When I told him this, Rick started sharing all he was grateful for, which was quite a bit. He was so grateful for the men's shelter that helped out the homeless, for his daughter keeping in touch with him, and for this barbershop that would cut homeless people's hair and give them clothes and shoes. I was so excited to hear all this and knew that those were two places I had to visit. He also said his AA meeting was in the building across the street. I love AA. I have fond memories of going to a gratitude AA meeting in Louisville the year before. The openness, freedom, and love people share within those walls are sacred. Rick told me that he would introduce me to the head of the men's shelter and the barbershop guys the next day. I told him I'd meet him at the AA meeting and then we could go visit with the others.

Before Rick and I said goodbye that day, he agreed to shoot a gratitude video with me. It was very honest and beautiful, and I felt special for just being there. There is a lot to say about someone who has nothing but is still so grateful.

The following day I got up and went to the coffee shop to work on the website. When I went to places like that, I would usually end up meeting someone nice and chatting, talking about gratitude, and possibly getting a video. People were kind and warm, and I really felt at peace in busy spots.

Then I walked over to the AA meeting spot to meet Rick and go to the meeting. I waited outside until one minute before they started and there was no Rick to be found. I thought since I was there I should go in. I sat down. There were around sixteen of us. I introduced myself. What I remember about this experience was that we all hugged each other and that the people were very nice. This was a safe place and it felt we all were grateful to be there. This was my second AA meeting. It reminded me of the gratitude AA meeting in Louisville. An AA meeting is a great place to get perspective and find appreciation.

After the meeting was over, an hour or so later, I left. Rick was in the parking lot. He explained why he was late and introduced me to Amanda. Apparently, she hadn't been on the streets that long, and he tried to look out for her when he could. I asked Amanda if she would shoot a little interview and share what she was grateful for. She was very kind and shared a powerful and beautiful moment with me. She said she was grateful for God. I asked her if she could tell me about a person who was physically in her life. I wanted her to share a person, not a holy being.

She then said she was grateful for her friend, Solo. I asked if there was a specific reason she thought of Solo. She said that he made her smile whenever they saw each other. Smile. How often have I taken for granted the many people in my life who have made me smile or given me a smile? Smiles manifest smiles, and there are people in life that give this gift freely all day long. We should give thanks to those people.

Rick and I headed to the Greater Cincinnati Homeless Coalition. It was a brisk ten-minute walk in this cold afternoon. Rick was easy to be around. I never felt like he wanted to take advantage of me. He was appreciative of the company and wanted to show off the people and organizations that had helped him out. This was a wonderful arrangement.

We walked into the Coalitions building and Rick asked if we could speak to Dr. Mark. We introduced ourselves, and I explained why I was there and what my website was all about. I asked if he would share what he was grateful for and tell me more about the Greater Cincinnati Homeless Coalition.

This organization did so much for the homeless people in Cincinnati. They had a magazine called Street Vibes that informed people what they were doing locally and shared different homeless people's stories. They also employed the homeless to sell the magazine on the streets. It was a fantastic reciprocal system.

Next, Rick and I walked to the barbershop, Incredible Creations. There, I met all the barbers. This was the place that gave Rick a haircut and new clothes and shoes. They made him feel like a person; they saw him and brought some normalcy to his life. They showed him love and he was very appreciative.

I got to interview Darren, one of the barbers. He shared his gratitude for his mother, which I related to. He also worked for the county, and he would go and cut the juveniles' hair before they would go to court. He'd talk to them and share his love of God. He would tell them they had choices to make. He would give them hope. He had also been in jail, so he could relate to how they felt. He showed them love by talking to them and cutting their hair, which was his passion. Darren had a lot to be grateful for.

Another time I was in a Mexican restaurant next to the lot where I had met Rick. I sat at the bar and started talking to the gentleman next to me, Frank. We had a lot in common. We were both grateful for our mothers. He shared with me some memories of his mother and expressed why he was most grateful for her. She had passed within the past year. He shared that Tuesday was always their day, that they would have lunch and dinner together, that it didn't matter if the meal was expensive or cheap, that it was their time together. He told me this with tears welling up in his eyes. The loss was obviously still present, but the gratitude was unfailing.

It's so easy to talk about gratitude. Common interests are found without any bullshit. I am grateful for these moments. These connections have impacted my journey.

I was using Tinder and met a young lady for a drink at a bar downtown, within walking distance from where I was staying. I enjoyed the conversation I had with this lady, but I don't remember her name and we never saw each other again. She did tell me that the bartender, Jason, was a grateful person and that I should interview him.

Jason shared gratitude for his mom. In the video, I asked him to name a few qualities he loved about his mom. He shot back with clarity and love. Then because we had talked before and he'd agreed that he would share the video with his mom, he told her that he loved her. It was beautiful.

COMPANIONS

"Animals are a gift from above for they truly define the words unconditional love."

Heather Wolf

I am so grateful for my cat Boog. She was so sweet and loving. I really miss how she would come and rub up against my leg and how she would sleep with me, cradled in my arm with her head on my shoulder.

Her name comes from when she was a baby. We had adopted her from the humane society. After she was with us for a week or two, she developed this wicked sinus infection. It was so bad that snot would block her nose and make it hard for her to breathe. Fortunately, the medicine the vet prescribed cleared it up. Because of this, she was always affectionately nicknamed Boog. I'm grateful for the time I had with Boog. Remembering these moments allows me to appreciate her more even though she is no longer with me.

ALWAYS TEACHING ME SOMETHING

FOR THE LOVE OF A DOG

by Gail Boenning

Gail is a longtime wife, mother, animal aficionado, and wanderer who devotes her life to curiosity, learning, and connecting. Like a river, she's forever flowing and changing.

Mid-February, winter climate, three-foot-high snowbanks, deep snow covering off road trails — my calf muscles are in constant spasm. My dog Mara — well, without hunting or baseball, she's sullen, bored, occasionally naughty and completely unfocused... despite all of that, there is light underneath the door — lessons to be learned.

When Mara was young, she was attacked by a neighborhood beagle — Tinker Bell. With a gaping hole in her left shoulder flesh, she was forced to sleepover at the emergency vet that Saturday night. On Sunday morning, she came home with twelve stitches, a plastic cone secured by a gauze bow around her neck, and a new behavior — leash aggression. Walking her tethered in the neighborhood became embarrassing and anxiety filled as she snapped and lunged at passing pooches. My sweet Labrador decided a good offense was her best defense. Once bitten, twice shy.

I researched — queried anything and everything written by Cesar Milan — and tried to remedy the situation. I learned I was most likely exacerbating the problem by tensing up every time I'd see another dog approaching. Mara can read my body language like a book. Without professional dog behaviorist help, I could not stem the problem. While walking in the neighborhood, Mara and I became a hot mess at the sight of another dog.

What did I do?

Of course I wasn't going to spend good money to hire a dog behaviorist! I adopted avoidance behavior. Mara and I began walking at odd hours when it was most likely we'd not come across other dogs. When I'd catch sight of another happy owner/pooch duo approaching, Mara and I would pivot and go another direction. What had been a treat — walking off leash on a nature trail — became our norm. Our daily half hour walk blossomed into a car ride with a romp of freedom on marsh or woodland paths. I've no complaints, because our daily commune with nature has been a blessing to us both.

Circling back to our current winter conditions though, we have a choice. I can wear my tennis shoes, click on Mara's plum, frayed leash and hit the subdivision roadways or, slip on my snow pants, lace up my winter boots and slog through nature's winter coat. We've been doing a bit of both.

Yesterday, on our slow, stop / pee / walk five feet / stop / pee / walk ten feet / stop / pee / walk seven feet-you get the idea walk, Mara stopped on a dime two houses before Tinker Bell's. I've no idea if the dog still lives there. It's been over a year since we walked past the fairy-not a fairy's house. Last winter, under similar weather conditions, that dog shot out of its garage like a missile programmed for Mara. I dropped Mara's leash, intercepted the beagle, picked it up and stood there dumbfounded. The owner was aware and came to get the snarling, wriggling dog from my arms. I acted all polite and oh, no problem, but that's not really what I felt. Why do I do that?

Anyhow, when Mara stopped yesterday, I gave a tug on her collar and firmly said, "C'mon! The garage door is down. Tinker Bell's not out." Have I mentioned Mara can be pretty stubborn? She was not budging no matter how grumpy I sounded.

Again, there were choices. I could — a.) Turn around and go back the way we came, which was double the distance of going past, or — b.) figure out how to get Mara to walk by Tinker Bell's house.

Not wanting to stop / pee / walk five feet / stop / pee / walk ten feet / stop / pee / walk seven feet-you get the idea for double the distance, I recognized I had to change my tactics and behavior. Forceful bullying was not getting me anywhere with Mara.

So here's what I did — I changed my behavior so that she could change hers.

I adopted my high pitched, happy voice. I pulled a treat from my pocket. I beseeched her to do her puppy prance. I told her what a good girl she is and promised we'd find her tennis ball when we got home.

It worked.

We went forward instead of back.

That dog of mine — she's the best teacher.

GRATEFUL

by Noosha Ravaghi

Noosha Ravaghi is an author and a copy editor.

I'm grateful
for the three angels who,
for over a decade,
have been by my side.
I'm grateful
for how they have loved me.
I'm grateful
because they have brought me joy,
taught me to be present,
played with me,
eaten with me,
walked with me,
slept with me,
kept me warm.
I'm grateful
for my companions
because they have protected me,
comforted me,
stayed up with me all night,
waited for me all day.
I'm grateful
for my dogs who,
day after day,
have licked my wounds,
shown me how to love,
motivated me to get back up,
been my best friends,

helped me find my true self,
made me become a better me.
I'm grateful
for every look,
for every kiss,
for every head tilt,
for every tail wag,
for every breath.
I'm grateful
for every moment
my dogs have honored me
with their presence.

I AM GRATEFUL FOR

THE UNCONDITIONAL LOVE OF A PET!

by Elizabeth Hartigan, The Gratitude Girl

Elizabeth Hartigan is an author, speaker, and gratitude & manifestation coach known as The Gratitude Girl. She discovered gratitude after being diagnosed with cancer two decades ago and healed herself naturally. She resides in Florida with her new pup Winston and partner Krish.

My life has been so incredibly blessed to experience unconditional love by my bundle of joy, Sterling, who entered my life September 9, 2002.

I had visited countless shelters and pet adoption centers and, after months of searching, I still could not find the dog I envisioned in my heart. I was starting to lose hope: I found tons of sweet dogs, all available for adoption, but I knew that they were not my guy.

One morning while I was getting ready, I received an intuitive nudge, the phrase ABC kept repeating itself over and over in my head. I wasn't quite sure what that meant. So I googled ABC and lo and behold, there was an ABC Animal Benefit Center, a no-kill shelter in Arizona. I immediately called them and asked what seemed like a totally normal question at the time. "Do you have a nine-month-old male Schnauzer or Westie who is potty trained, playful, and a lap dog size?"

And to my excitement, her response was, "Why yes we do! He was dropped off at 8pm last night. Did his owners tell you that he could be found here?" I couldn't tell her how I knew he was there so simply said, "I just had a feeling."

Immediately, I jumped into the car and raced across town to go meet my puppy! I was so certain that he was the one, that I offered to pay her via credit card on the spot. She assured me that she would hold him for me, until I could arrive.

As I walked into the adoption center, I was led to the waiting room. It felt like an eternity, until the door opened and a little, shy puppy slowly looked out of the door of the room he was being kept in. He was so afraid that, as he left the room, he was literally creeping against the wall. Once he saw me, he came running towards me, as though he recognized me. He plowed into me, kissed every inch of my face, grabbed the stuffed panda bear that I had brought him, and ran to the front door, squeaking his toy and staring back at me. The shelter owner said, "I think he wants to go home with you." I already had my check made out, I handed it to her, and Sterling and I left within ten minutes of my arrival.

From that day on, Sterling was my shadow and followed my every move. He would sit on my feet while I typed, he lay next to me while sleeping. If I moved even an inch to get more room or cool off, he moved with me. He would wake up in the middle of the night to lick or kiss my nose to make sure I was well before going back to sleep.

I miss his presence each and every day, and I am eternally grateful for the unconditional love and extreme joy that he brought into my life.

A few of my favorite things about Sterling:

He would spin around to get his tail, which made me laugh hysterically. He would then stop to look at me to be sure I was enjoying his rampage, and then immediately spin in the opposite direction as if to unwind.

One of his favorite things was when we played hide and seek. If I hid, he would look for me and didn't stop looking until he found me. He loved it when I hid cookies in plastic Easter eggs around the yard. He would pop them open and grab the treat inside, then bring me the empty egg shells to do it again!

On days when I felt sick, he would lay next to me on the sofa. Never leaving my side. He could sense where there might be pain in my body, and would lie exactly where the pain resided, blessing me with heat and puppy healing, which always made me feel better.

Without a doubt, my life is richer and fuller because he was in it!

I have the ability to love deeper because of his love. He was one of the greatest teachers of my life, and I will be eternally grateful for his love, for his life, and that the universe so graciously brought us together.

Gratitude Challenge!

What beloved pet or animal has blessed your life?

How is your life richer or fuller, thanks to the unconditional love of a pet?

What animals have blessed your life with their presence?

How can you bless the life of an animal today?

MIS MEJORES AMIGOS

by Rocío del Mar

Tuve la fortuna de crecer en una familia en la cual me enseñaron que el amor y respeto por los animales era sagrado. De niña en mi casa no solo teníamos como mascotas a gatos y perros, también tuvimos conejos, pájaros, peces, loros, pollos que luego fueron gallos y hasta las hormigas fueron mis amigas (aunque no creo que ellas lo supieran), y yo las ayudaba a que se comieran las plantas del jardín de mi abuelito, así que en esta ocasión quiero rendir un homenaje y toda mi gratitud a todos los animales que han sido parte de mi vida a través de Katty y Pachita.

Katty llegó a mi casa cuando yo tenía diez años y era tan pequeñita que ni siquiera podía abrir los ojos y cabía en una de las manos de mi mamá, recuerdo que la alimentábamos con un tetero de bebé y que se despertaba a la madrugada a pedir su comida, literalmente como un bebé. Siempre era la primera en salir a recibirme cuando yo llegaba del colegio, siempre moviendo su colita, demostrando cuanta alegría le daba el verme regresar a casa; fue mi amiga por 14 años, crecimos juntas y compartimos hermosos momentos, aunque debo admitir que en algunas ocasiones peleábamos y yo siempre salía perdiendo, puesto que sus mordiscos eran más fuertes que mis regaños.

De Katty aprendí que la nobleza de los perritos es infinita, que por más castigos que pudiera imponerle, nunca iba a dejar de ser la primera en darme la bienvenida cada vez que regresaba a la casa, que su lealtad no conocía límites y que darnos a conocer su agradecimiento y darnos su amor, era su misión más importante.

Luego de la partida de Katty, mi familia decidió no tener mascotas y así estuvimos por casi 8 años, hasta que un día una decisión ajena a nuestra voluntad nos hizo cambiar de idea y esa decisión la tomó Pachita, quién llegó a nuestras vidas por una ventana y como siempre suelo decir, desde ese preciso momento fuimos adoptados por ella, quien nos escogió como su familia. Ella es literalmente la reina de mi casa y nosotros somos sus súbditos, que estamos prestos a cumplir sus deseos y caprichos. Es la gata más inteligente que conozco, aunque creo que esto lo deben de pensar la mayoría de los que tenemos un amigo de 4 patas en nuestras vidas sobre su respectiva mascota. Pachita aprendió a tratarnos de una forma particular y de acuerdo con nuestra personalidad, por ejemplo es dulce con mi mamá quién es su humana favorita y caprichosa con mi papá quien hace todo lo que ella desea.

De Pachita aprendí que el amor por un gato se entrega sin esperar retribuciones, que por el simple hecho de que sea una mascota, no puedo consentirla cuando yo quiera, a Pachita la acaricio cuando ella lo permite, en caso contrario mis manos y brazos sufren las consecuencias.

Estoy muy agradecida con Katty, con Pachita y con todas las mascotas que de una u otra forma han sido parte de mi vida, gracias por la compañía, por cuidarme, por enseñarme tantas cosas, por hacerme ver la vida de forma diferente, pero sobretodo gracias por tanto, tanto amor.

Creo que no puedo cerrar este escrito de una mejor manera que recordando una frase célebre de Anatole France: "Hasta que no hayas amado a un animal, una parte de tu alma estará dormida"

Rocío del Mar

I was fortunate to grow up in a family in which I was taught that love and respect for animals were sacred. As a child, in my house, we not only had cats and dogs as pets, we also had rabbits, birds, fish, parrots, chicks that later became roosters; even ants were my friends (although I don't think they knew it), and I I helped them eat the plants in my grandfather's garden, so this time I want to pay tribute and all my gratitude to all the animals that have been part of my life through Katty and Pachita.

Katty came to my house when I was ten years old. She was so little that she couldn't even open her eyes, and she could fit in one of my mother's hands. I remember that we fed her with a baby bottle and that she would wake up at dawn to ask for food literally like a baby.

She was always the first to come out to greet me when I came home from school, always wagging her little tail, showing how much joy it gave her to see me return home. She was my friend for 14 years. We grew up together and shared beautiful moments, although I must admit that on some occasions we fought, and I always lost, since her bites were stronger than my scolding.

From Katty I learned that the nobility of dogs is infinite, that no matter how much punishment I could impose on her, she would never stop being the first to welcome me every time I returned home. There were no limits to her loyalty and her gratitude; and giving us her love was her most important mission.

After Katty's departure, my family decided not to have pets, and we stayed that way for almost eight years, until one day a decision beyond our control made us change our mind. That decision was made by Pachita, who came into our lives because of a window, and, as I always say, from that precise moment we were adopted by her; she chose us as her family. She is literally the queen of my house and we are her subjects, ready to fulfill her wishes and whims. She is the most intelligent cat I know. Although I think that most of us who have a four-legged friend in our lives must think that about our respective pet. Pachita learned to treat us in a particular way and according to our personality; for example, she is sweet with my mother who is her favorite human and capricious with my father who does everything she wants.

From Pachita I learned that love for a cat is given without waiting for retribution, that just because it is a pet, I cannot pamper it whenever I want. I caress Pachita when she allows it; otherwise, my hands and arms suffer the consequences.

I am very grateful to Katty, to Pachita, and to all the pets that, in one way or another, have been part of my life. Thank you for the company, for taking care of me, for teaching me so many things, for making me see life in a different way, but above all thank you so much for so much love.

I think I cannot close this writing in a better way than by recalling a famous phrase from Anatole France: "Until you have loved an animal, a part of your soul will be asleep."

Rocío del Mar

GRATITUDE IS LOVERLY

WITH ELIZA DOOLITTLE

by Hilary Russo

Hilary Russo is a health/wellness journalist, Certified Integrative Nutrition Holistic Health Coach and Certified Havening Techniques Practitioner. Her podcast "HILlistically Speaking" focuses on empowering conversations of transformation from trauma to triumph through health, healing and humor.

When I talk about my sweet kitty Eliza, I often say we saved each other. Eliza came into my life during a difficult time. My relationship was struggling, I was in the middle of a career change and I had lost my father a few years prior. I felt a loneliness and uncertainty that couldn't be explained. Thinking about bringing a pet into my life was the last thing on my mind. I wasn't sure I had the emotional bandwidth to nurture anything else, let alone myself. But Miss Eliza Doolittle had other plans.

I remember it was a cold Thanksgiving Day in North Carolina. I was living in the Carolinas at the time and had just wrapped a lovely holiday dinner with friends. Driving back home, my eyes fixated on a tiny calico puff in a hotel parking lot. Cowering near a storm drain, her little mouth gaped opened as if it were a cry for help. I understood her loneliness and uncertainty as I passed by, only to quickly do a U-Turn. Within seconds I found her under a car and tempted her with turkey leftovers. The rest is history. I found her in a gutter, so the name fits. Theatre lovers will get the My Fair Lady reference. A once wet and matted kitten became quite an aristo-CAT.

For fifteen years, this cat has been my little shadow. Together we've lived in multiple states, been through a couple relationships, witnessed some births as well as a few deaths, and even shot a commercial together. Yes. She's the Blue Buffalo cat food commercial kitty. I'm just there for moral support. All kidding aside, this beautiful being has given me so much, even when I felt I had so little. It's amazing how much can be packed into eight pounds of a purring machine. But the biggest gift she has given me is love. Always love. Eliza has taught me how easy it is to find joy in the moment and be in a constant state of gratitude. She's a reminder to be present and relax. All she knows is love, because love is all there is. Seems like the purrrfect formula for living your life "loverly."

MY KITTY CAT GRACIE JEAN

by Al Palmore

My story starts with my daughter, Jeannie, and my son, Chris. After the passing of my wife, their mom, over six years ago, my children knew I was a lonely man, so they both thought it would be a good idea for Dad to get a pet. I didn't want one until after a year and half of being alone. My daughter got me a puppy. He was cute, warm, and fuzzy, but very needy. If you didn't hold him, he would cry, bark, and jump up on you. He only lasted ten days with me. I know my daughter was disappointed when I told her the dog wouldn't work.

It wasn't long after returning the dog that both my daughter and son had another idea for their dad. How about a kitten? I was willing to think about it. They told me that there were a lot of kittens at the Humane Society. I told them to pick out three kittens and I would choose one. The day came for me to go and choose one of the cats. I walked into where the cats lived, and after they pointed out the three cats, I made my choice, and took a black and white little kitten home.

Now, five years later, I am so in love with and so grateful for Gracie Jean. We have grown to be best friends. She is a faithful friend to me. She looks out the front window to watch when I come home. After seeing me she takes off to the front door to greet me. She follows me everywhere I go in the house; it doesn't matter where I go, including the bathroom. She has me wrapped around her little paw. I am so grateful that I have someone to talk to and hold and pet. When she looks up at me, I just melt.

In the beginning, she didn't have much of a voice, but now you can hear her talk no matter where she is. I am grateful to God for providing me with the best kitty cat on planet earth!

Gracie is a wonderful friend to me. I hope I am one for her. I am forever grateful that God brought this amazing, sweet, sensitive, kind, warm, and fuzzy creature into my life. The joy that she brings has helped me to take on life. Just knowing that she gets excited to see me pull up in the driveway and how she greets me at my front door makes it a little easier to come home.

Even though we don't speak each other's language, the body language between us is so real and beautiful. Having a pet is like having a child. Pets truly are part of the family, and life just wouldn't be the same without them.

JULIEM

by Edinho

Las mascotas dentro de un hogar se vuelven un miembro más de la familia, para muchas personas incluso son como hijos, en este corto ensayo hablaré de mi perrito con nombre Juliem que tiene 6 años, primero quiero contarles que es de raza Coker Spaniel Inglés, y su nombre hace referencia al rey Juliem de los pingüinos de Madagascar, le puse ese nombre porque es considerado el rey de la casa, sus padres también fueron de su misma raza, cabe mencionar que su papá también fue mi mascota y se llamaba Luigi, como el amigo de Mario Bross.

Este pequeño y cariñoso perro es muy querido en nuestro hogar, como a todo perro le gusta salir a la calle apenas se abre la puerta del garaje, un par de veces nos hemos descuidado al abrir la puerta y por esta razón ha sufrido diversos accidentes. Fue golpeado muy fuerte por un vehículo, este golpe lo dejó postrado aproximadamente por un mes, sin poder caminar, pero con nuestros cuidados y medicamentos se recuperó.

Se atoró con huesos, lo que le produjo problemas intestinales, pero igual se recuperó. En otra circunstancia tomó veneno para ratas, pero con un lavado estomacal y cuidados, se volvió a recuperar. En otra ocasión, tuvo una caída de cinco metros por la ruptura de un domo, y salió ileso.

En todos los accidentes que ha sufrido Juliem, mi familia y yo hemos estado muy tristes, pensando que ya iba a morir, pero mi perro nos ha demostrado que es muy fuerte, recuperándose exitosamente de todos los accidentes que ha tenido. Esto nos ha llevado a considerar que Juliem tiene alma de gato con varias vidas.

Actualmente mi perro se encuentra bien y es feliz, es muy noble, cariñoso y juguetón, yo lo considero como mi hermano canino, por la vida de él y la manera de cómo llegó a mi vida, y nos sigue acompañando, estoy muy agradecido; además considero que las mascotas son seres mágicos que llenan de amor nuestras vidas.

Pets within a home become another member of the family. For many people they are even like children. In this short essay, I will talk about my puppy named Juliem who is six years old. First, I want to tell you that he is an English Cocker Spaniel breed, and his name refers to King Juliem of the penguins of Madagascar. I gave him that name because he is considered the king of the house. His parents were also of the same race, and it is worth mentioning that his father was also my pet and his name was Luigi, as Super Mario's brother.

This small and affectionate dog is very loved in our home. As every dog likes to go outside as soon as the garage door opens, a couple of times we have been careless when opening the door, and for this reason he has suffered various accidents. Once he was hit very hard by a vehicle; this blow left him unable to walk for about a month, but with our care and medications he recovered. Another time, he ate bones which he couldn't break, and it gave him intestinal problems, but he still recovered. In another circumstance, he took rat poison, but with a stomach wash and care, he recovered again. On another occasion, he fell five meters from a ruptured dome, and was unharmed.

In all the accidents that Juliem has suffered, my family and I have been very sad, thinking that he was going to die, but my dog has shown us that he is very strong, and he has recovered from all the accidents. This has led us to consider that Juliem has the soul of a cat with several lives.

Currently my dog is healthy and happy, he is very noble, affectionate and playful. I consider him as my canine brother because of his life and the way he came into my life.

He continues to accompany us and I am very grateful. I believe that pets are magical beings that fill our lives with love.

Edinho

AT 7:47

"If you could give credit and thanks to one person in your life that you DON'T give enough credit or thanks to, who would that be?"
Chris Schembra

A short while ago, I went for a lap around the old park. The weather was nice and I hadn't jogged in the park in many months. I checked my podcast app to see what I could listen to, and I ended up choosing Big Questions with Cal Fussman.

I was looking at his podcast lineup, and the word *gratitude* caught my eye. I chose that one and started my run. He introduced a man named Chris Schembra. Chris explained he had been hosting what are essentially gratitude dinners for the past five years, and he had connected over 400,000 people with these dinners. He started a business that catered to companies to host these dinners. He had just released a book called *Gratitude and Pasta*. His pasta was what originally sprung the idea of having the dinner party.

I got back from my jog and decided I needed to reach out to this Chris. On the podcast he mentioned how he could be reached. I sent a short message letting him know I had heard him on the podcast and I had started my journey after my mom had died of cancer several years back. He responded the next day and invited me to a dinner party over Zoom two nights later. This guy was using Zoom video conferences and making real connections happen. The meeting started and several of us guys were on a few minutes early. Chris was playing some chill party music as we were waiting. He explained that we were waiting for around ten more people to show up and that most people popped on at about the time to start, 7:47.

Many more people arrived. Now the screen was full of people. Chris asked us to all mute ourselves so that he could lead the dinner party. A dinner party was a fun idea even if very few people were eating. He told us he was happy that we all showed up and he knew it would be a magical time. He went on to explain a little about how this all got started. He had been producing a play in Italy. Then when he got back to NYC, he went into a depression from the lack of connection. He started making this pasta sauce in his home and decided to invite some friends over to try it out. He wanted their feedback. He continued doing this week after week and then something amazing started to happen. He started asking this question about gratitude to get people to open up and connect.

He asked all of us to say our name and one word to describe how we were feeling at this exact moment. When it was my turn, I introduced myself and where I was from, and I said I was excited. We all went around and did this. It was a fun and easy way for everyone to be introduced and participate. Next, he said that we were all going to be put in a breakout room with one other person. In this room, we would have a total of five minutes to talk. We would each say hi and explain why we used the word we used to describe how we were feeling.

I was put in a room with Holly, Chris's girlfriend. Her word was "anxious." She explained to me that they were living in NYC and thinking of getting a car and getting out of town for a while and this feeling had occurred. She thought it was a good thing that she had noticed this feeling.

She then asked me if my word was "excited." I answered that it was. I was excited because my mission for the past several years was inspiring gratitude. I explained the chain of events that had led me to that moment. She then went on to ask how I got involved in the gratitude journey. I then went into my story and how it had all gotten started.

The time at this point clicked on the screen that we'd be kicked back into the main group within a minute. She urged me to continue the story and I did. When I got to the point where my mom died, Holly was totally taken in with my story. It was great to share and connect with her.

Then we got sent back to the main group. Chris at this point welcomed us back and asked if anyone wanted to share what they learned from their time with the other. Holly spoke up and said that she'd like to share. She then went on to explain what I had told her smiling the whole time.

In the next part of the dinner, we got into groups of three and answered Chris's gratitude question: "If you could give credit and thanks to one person in your life that you DON'T give enough credit or thanks to, who would that be?"

One lady shared appreciation and love for her mother-in-law. The other person in the room was a guy who shared appreciation and love for a high school teacher. He stated that if it weren't for this teacher he wouldn't be who he was today and wouldn't have chosen the career that he was in.Then it was my turn, and my mind answered with the name Bill McGee. The best way to tell the rest of this story is to share the text message I shared with Bill the next day:

Good morning, Bill,

It's Chris Palmore.

I'm guessing it's been over five years since we got coffee at Starbucks off of Blankenbaker and Hurstbourne Ln.

I was asked a very powerful question last night: "If you could give credit or thanks to one person in your life that you DON'T give enough credit or thanks to, who would that be?"

This suddenly reminded me of you, Bill McGee.

Meeting you and you being who you are changed the course of my entire life for the better. I remember that you picked me up from my parents' house and took me to Arby's, that you were funny and had a laid back easy going honest feeling. I trusted you and felt that you cared about me, someone that you didn't know from Adam. (Look at me throwing in Biblical references.)

I felt comfortable enough with you to agree to go to Windy Gap and the rest is history. Wonderful friends and memories! I don't think I would have learned how to play the guitar if it wasn't for the club, and I have great memories of Barney and me practicing songs at his house. The memories go on and on.

I still talk with Rick from time to time and what a gift he has been in my life. Again, thanks to your kind heart and compassion.

I was also asked to name a few qualities that I think of when I think of you: Fun, Honesty, Trust, Love, Laughter, Being Present, Happiness

I hope you are well. I just wanted to thank you with all of my heart and let you know that I was thinking about you.

In Gratitude,

Chris

Bill responded:

Can't tell you how this touched my soul.

I remember Arby's like it was yesterday.

This simple question asked in an online setting sparked a memory. That memory allowed me to express gratitude to someone I had not. It's a powerful sauce Chris is cooking up, and I'm so grateful for his friendship, experience, and connections.

DEAR UNCLE GASTON

by Nika Paradis

Dear Uncle Gaston,

My fondest childhood memories are all the times you looked after me. I don't remember ever thanking you for being the best babysitter in the world, but please know that I will forever remain grateful for you and for the time you spent with me. You were the coolest uncle a girl could wish for. I had so much fun with you that I didn't want you to ever leave.

I always thought of you as my older brother. When I didn't know how to play a game, you showed me how and practiced with me. When I was being bullied at school, you taught me how to stand up to the bullies. When I was having a bad time at home, you took me to the beach... and bribed me with ice cream so that I wouldn't tell Dad you brought a date.

Do you remember the chili pepper incident? I was nine, and you came over to stay with me. I was sitting at the dining table finishing my fish and vegetables, and I was eating really spicy chili peppers on the side. I had gotten used to eating extremely spicy food at summer camp, where their idea of a healthy snack was a baguette sandwich with nothing but harissa, but you didn't know that. The way I was biting into those peppers without reacting to how hot they were made you think that they were sweet, so you picked one up and put it in your mouth. Immediately, your whole face turned red and you seemed to be choking. I just sat there and giggled. When you finally caught your breath, you were shocked that I wasn't burning and looked at Dad. He told you about my summer camp snacks.

Do you remember when you had your motorcycle accident? I was so worried about you. It took you months to recover. It made me sad that I couldn't visit you every day. You probably didn't know this, but I thought of you all the time. I hated seeing you in pain. I hoped your leg would heal and things would get back to the way they had been before the accident.

Do you remember the pranks we pulled on my dad? I still remember some of those and laugh. You were the only person who knew all my secrets while I was growing up. I have a lot of memories of our time together, and even though we have lived on different continents for some time now, you have always been in my thoughts, and I have always cherished those memories. I am grateful for you.

Your Grateful Niece, N

A GRATITUDE LETTER

by Medea Kalantar

Medea Kalantar is the award-winning author of Honeycake Book Series.

Every day I start my day off with gratitude to God for giving me another day to be alive and for allowing me to serve, influence, and transform this planet for the higher good. I give thanks for my family, soul family, friends, all the beautiful souls I cross paths with, and all the frontline workers who work so hard to make our lives a little bit easier. But there is one person I never thank... myself.

So here I go!

To start off with, I am so proud of you. Life hasn't been easy on you, my love, but despite it all, you have managed to keep your head up with grace and rise up like a Phoenix, stronger than before.

Be proud of all your challenges, for they have transformed you into the beautiful soul you've become.

Don't take everything to heart, and try to not let others get you down. Most of the time, it has nothing to do with you and everything to do with the other person. When people hurt you, have patience and compassion, and try to understand their side of the story. Forgive them. Learn from those lessons, and then let go of the negativity. Not everything is always how it appears.

You are perfect in every way, especially with your flaws. Embrace the things that make you unique.

Even though you think you are broken, there is so much beauty in your pain. Also, you're really not as broken as you think you are. You are stronger than anything or anyone that has tried to tear you down. You are a VICTOR, not a VICTIM. So with that, try not to be so hard on yourself; you are doing the best you can.

Create a meaningful life for yourself, one you can be proud of. Promise me you will make the most of it all. Never let anyone get in the way of your goals in life. More importantly, never give up on your passions and your dreams. Do not waste your time on people who do not believe in you. You don't need anyone like that in your life. Only surround yourself with people who encourage and inspire you.

You deserve the world and even a little more. You are smart. You are beautiful. You are enough. You are everything. You are all.

You are so strong, my love. You have been through a lot and come out on the winning end. The world has tried to break you, but you never let it.

Thank your past, for it has made you into a better person today.

Not everyone you have met is meant to stay around forever. People will leave you. You will also leave others. People will disappoint you, and all you can do is learn to appreciate them for what they have taught you.

Thank the people who have stayed. Fill the spaces of the ones who have gone. More importantly, gracefully let go of the things and people that are not meant for you. Accept things the way they are.

Thank you for being so tough and never giving up. You inspire others and you lift them up. Stay strong. Stand up tall. Be more beautiful than ever. Make them wonder how you do it.

You know you deserve the world; now go get it.

Thank you Medea. I love you, and I'm so grateful for you.

FRIENDS

by A. Allan

From an early age, we are surrounded by people; family, peers and friends. When it comes to the latter, we often tend to think that by mere grace they are obliged to be with us, to hang out with us and to put up with us.

It is not an easy task to stand us.

We do not take into account that sometimes we can not even stand ourselves. But they, those so-called friends, they keep up with us no matter what.

And we, we act as if it were normal for people to care for us with no conditioning whatsoever.

We are all special, but in a world where it has become so hard for that to be recognized among people, we must be aware that friends have done so when it comes to thinking of us as exceptional.

Not having noticed that is to live in the shadows.

As for me, well, as time has passed by, and my struggles have not been faced alone, I must say, I am enlightened since I have become aware of what a good friend is.

And for that, I just wanted to say:

"Let us be grateful for that premise and let us enjoy being beholden to those friends!"

DEAR DAD

by Marc Levine

Dear Dad,

You're amazing. You keep going after all these years. You are the definition of resilience. You've survived cancer, a heart attack, and the deaths of wives, siblings, and a daughter.

You keep going. Thank you for continuing to keep on. It's given us a chance to settle into a very sweet and very loving relationship. I look forward to our calls and emails. It's amazing to see how good it feels to have you pick up the phone. I appreciate our jokes, talks about old movies, and how you listen when I have life challenges. You're always there.

Thank you for your willingness to change and grow in your late 80s. Thank you for seeing me in a new light.

Thank you for your caring for others. You are a model for looking out for thy neighbor as thy self.

Thanks for being an imperfect father... because I am certainly an imperfect son. Here's to new laughs, new discoveries, and a hug.

Love,
Marc

SELF LOVE

by Ifumi Ehigiator

Ifumi Ehigiator is a Nigerian writer and poet.

Once upon a time, when several parts of my body were treated like outcasts, I admired many peers of mine and sought to be like them. I felt like they had something I didn't. They seemed so perfect. Maybe it was my natural hair or not-very straight legs, which were often points of ridicule for me. A few people enjoyed being in my company. For the others, I was prepared to wear myself out in order to gain their approval. This was my plight for a few years. After escaping drowning in that sea of low self-esteem, I realized nothing makes anyone else better than me. Rather, we are all unique beings. Despite being mocked, I moved on and gradually began to struggle towards self consciousness and self love. There were those sincere enough to admire unique traits of mine. This proved to me that everyone is a two-sided coin. They have flaws and admirable traits alike. No one deserves to be humiliated. Self love and self consciousness, when in abundance, can positively impact life, all-round, and can also promote productivity. Today I must confess I am still on that journey but never again will I take the path I have abandoned. Good riddance to low self esteem and its baggage.

THE PSYCHOLOGY OF GRATITUDE

by Bobby Kountz

Bobby Kountz is an inspirationalist and the author of The Someday Solution.

In the spring of 1990, I was in my freshman year of college after completing five years in the United States Army. I didn't really see myself as a college student but since I had earned $26,500 for college, I thought it would be a good idea to at least give it a try.

I had no idea what I really wanted to be when I grew up, and since I still had a lot of growing up to do, I began my college career with an undeclared major. My first semester would focus on core curriculum requirements necessary for any degree.

One of my earliest challenges before enrolling in college was figuring out where to begin with mathematics. You see, I graduated from a vocational high school where I learned all about woodworking and I never really cared much for math. I was great with simple addition, subtraction, and measuring things, but beyond that, I didn't have much use for math.

The math placement exam is designed for one purpose: to most closely match the test taker with the appropriate level of math based on an understanding of math basics. My basics began at Math 95D. This meant I couldn't even think about Algebra until I was a sophomore. It was a huge blow to my already fragile ego and ever-present imposter syndrome feelings of not belonging...

I was in college not because I felt like I belonged, but because I felt like I had an obligation to at least give it a try even if I had no idea what I was doing. My first semester was an absolute disaster, not because I couldn't do the work, but because I had a secret. Even though I had gone into the military to straighten out my life, the truth was I had barely escaped serious circumstances related to my inability to carry out life without alcohol. I went into the military to get some discipline and to get clean and sober and for a while, it worked, until it didn't.

Finding myself free of the disciplined life of the military, it didn't take long for the downward spiral of alcoholism to kick in and take over again. I wasn't just an alcoholic either, I was a black out drunk, so much so that I still have huge gaps in my memory from the worst of times.

In that first semester there was one man who seemed more interested in my ability than I was. His name was Ray Rich and I've never taken the opportunity to formally thank him for the difference he made in my life that first semester. One day after class he asked me to stay behind. I think Mr. Rich looked at me as a social experiment. As a psychology professor, he had a deep desire to understand human behavior, and I believe mine perplexed him. I am forever grateful it did because he could have just as easily treated me like every other kid who performed poorly or failed to come to class, but instead he embraced me and he challenged me. He saw something in me that I had no idea existed. He saw something in me that had been lost to me for years. He saw potential, and his ability to see what I could not created a crack in the armor of indifference I cloaked myself in every day. My armor was a black leather jacket and a bad attitude, but underneath that artificial exterior, Ray Rich saw me, a scared and broken kid who had never dealt with the pain of a troubled childhood. He somehow knew "I" was still in there, and he made it his mission to reach me.

I remember him asking me what I was so angry about all the time and exactly who I thought I was punishing with my reckless behavior. Yes, he knew that I was coming to class drunk and that I rode a motorcycle to and from school. He also knew what a dangerous combination that was. As we talked and he got me to pay attention to him, I remember him asking me if I had any goals, aspirations, or dreams. I think I told him being able to make sense of my life might be a great place to start so psychology would probably be cool. I think he really liked my answer because he went to a filing cabinet and came back with a piece of what looked like parchment paper with a message on it about how all men dream but not equally.

I read the words on that piece of paper repeatedly and held on to it like a security blanket that semester. However, I still hadn't acknowledged what was eating me up inside, so instead of trying to deal with the pain, I tried to drown it. It was summer now and I was in between semesters. I remember waiting for my grades to come to find out how many classes I had failed. When they finally did come, I wasn't disappointed. I had done just as poorly as I had imagined, and, in an effort to numb the pain, I drank myself into a stupor until I finally passed out. When I awoke, the words of both Ray Rich and author T. E. Lawrence were waiting for me: "All men dream, but not equally. Those who dream by night in the dusty recesses of their minds, wake in the day to find that it was vanity: but the dreamers of the day are dangerous men, for they may act their dreams with open eyes, to make them possible."

Ray Rich taught me not only psychology, but also to dream. I still am!

Ray Rich, I will be forever grateful!

In Gratitude,

Bobby Kountz

A LETTER

by Nancy Liu Lan

Dear Kong Kong and Nai Nai,

It has taken Covid 19 for me to write you a thank you letter. I'm sitting on the balcony, my new office facing a white Buddha with a string of precious stones like the ones in Rain Flower Terrace in Nanjing where you were first buried.

Nai Nai, you wouldn't be allowed to practice any religion in modern China. So you've shown all of us a devoted life Buddha would have approved of. You smiled every day even when the Red Guards stormed into our home and threatened you with a knife, asking where the gold bars were hiding. You never raised your voice at my brothers and me. You always helped the neighbours with housework. You accompanied Kong Kong to the Re-education Camp. You worked in the fields with your feet bound. You taught me to focus on the positive and be more selfless. I went to University of Hong Kong to study Buddhist Studies and learnt to cultivate positive emotions and embrace death.

Kong Kong, you've given all of us abundance. You've shown me what unconditional love is all about. You've arranged for my parents, my two brothers and me to leave Nanjing in June 1973 for Hong Kong. You endured loneliness in the last years of your life so we could attend universities in the US instead of being sent to the countryside in China. There's always a bitter smile on my face whenever I mention you died on March 8, 1978, on Women's Day. The modern China has changed you to respect women. You wanted me to study in the US and work at UN to bring world peace. You were sorry that you didn't let your only daughter study in the UK when she was young. You and she believed education is the key to change the world. I'm sorry I didn't become a diplomat for China. I never thanked you two for my upbringing and I'll do my best to make you proud of your youngest granddaughter. The image of you practicing Tai Chi in front of the train in 1973 shall always stay with me.

I'll always keep the positive energy with you two looking after me from above. May your love bless our world. Thank you, Liu Guo Jun and Liu Ju Xiu.

THANKS, JERK!

by Chris Davis

My former boss was a jerk. A real jerk. He was a guy you simply could not trust and someone who was only out for himself. He was slippery, slimy, and sneaky, like a reptile or cave creature. He used his power for wickedness and he pretended to be helping you grow or improve, but he was really using you for his own gain. He was, by far, the worst leader I have ever worked for in my 30 years in technology.

We got put together as a result of my taking on an international role at my former high tech company. I was offered a role to guide a significant portion of our operations in Taiwan. He had just been assigned a leadership role in the US that would oversee my organization as well as several other groups. On the one hand, it was a great move for me because it allowed me to start a new life outside of the US and experience the true beauty and culture of Taiwan while helping to grow and lead an organization. The people and the lifestyle here are amazing, and I can't think of a better place to live. On the other hand, working for him turned out to be incredibly stressful and difficult, and it ended up being the worst possible move for my career. In fact, it was the final stage of a twenty-year journey at this company. In twenty years, I had garnered a reasonable amount of respect, success and responsibility, and it came to an end working for this guy.

Life under his command was torture, really, constantly being second guessed and micromanaged from a distance with no consideration for my experience, my organization, or my own health and welfare. I was at his beck and call 24 hours a day, 12 hours a day on my side of the world and 12 hours a day from his US perch. It was a nightmare in retrospect.

I am two years removed from that experience and, as strange as it sounds, I can honestly say that I need to tell him "thank you." Thank you for being the catalyst that propelled me to where I am today. His sheer awesomeness at being unreasonable, untrustworthy, and inhuman was instrumental in giving me the perspective to understand what's really important and valuable in life.

After leaving my old job, I decided to continue to live and work in Taiwan. I wouldn't have a big salary anymore, but I would gain so much more in terms of quality of life. I decided to pursue a career as an independent consultant and freelancer. I leverage all of my experience and background from so many years in technology to help individuals and small startups navigate business and organizational challenges. I also spend time just connecting with people from around the world, and I travel extensively in Asia because of my proximity. Japan, Korea, Thailand, Vietnam, Indonesia, and the Philippines are all quite close and accessible, and I have been given such a wonderful opportunity to see the world and experience new cultures.

I frequently reflect on my tumultuous time with my old boss and marvel at how it enabled me to have such a rewarding and much simpler life. I was blind to these joys because of the pressure, stress and inhospitable environment created by my former boss. So I have to offer up my sincere thanks to him, and although it was the toughest journey of my life, I am grateful that I persisted and survived because it put me in the best place I have ever been.

DEAR GRANDMA

by Teddy Droseros

Dear Grandma,

You raised me, and I don't think I ever really said thank you. I'll never forget our trips on the city bus to the bank and to get hot dogs. I'll never forget the cookies we made together from scratch, and how you would yell at me for eating so much raw dough. I'm sorry if I've been out of touch the past several years. Things got really intense with Mom, and I didn't have the space for much else in my life. You're now 97 years old! It doesn't look like you'll be around for much longer, and I'm really grateful you got to meet the future mother of my kids this past summer. I'm grateful I got to see and feel my mom's energy within you after she passed. I love you, Grandma. Thank you for everything. I'm not sure if I'll ever really know how much of an impact you had on my life. I'll NEVER forget our times on 36th Street together. I hope to see you again before your soul is finally at peace and with Mom and Grandpa.

Thank you, Grandma.

Love,

Your grandson Teddy

ENCOURAGEMENT, SUPPORT, FRIENDSHIP, AND GRATITUDE

by Bobby Kountz

Bobby Kountz is an inspirationalist and the author of The Someday Solution.

I was right back where I had started before I went into the military; I was in jail for reckless driving. I remember thinking I would probably be better off dead... Fortunately for me, God had other ideas and I somehow found the courage to call my sister to see if she would consider helping me. She did. I am so grateful that my sister was able to see something in me that I could not yet see in myself.

As I stood at the crossroads, I knew I would either end up in prison or dead, so on the 4th of July 1990, with the help of the god of my understanding, I declared my independence. I asked that the desire to drink be taken away, and it was. I asked that I be spared any more struggles with being able to just say no, and I was. It was nothing short of a miracle. As part of the deal, I promised to make a real difference in the world, and I have tried to live up to that promise every day of my life since.

College, clean and sober, was a completely different experience, but not right away; it took a little time, and it also took the encouragement of some friends and a couple professors, who once again saw something in me that I was not yet ready to see in myself.

Larry Tomlinson was a professor of philosophy. He taught me to question everything. He started with the syllabus of his very own class. I remember him telling all of us that everything we needed to know to be successful in his class was in the syllabus. He also said that instead of believing him we should read the syllabus to see if he was telling us the truth. I think his syllabus was the only one I ever read from cover to cover in college. It was a great lesson.

Prior to meeting Mr. Tomlinson, I had never been taught to think critically. My life was never the same after his class, and his teaching prepared me for the lessons I would learn in 1991 from a legendary business philosopher named Jim Rohn. I am forever grateful for the lessons Mr. Tomlinson shared with me, but I never formally expressed just how much his words meant to me.

Mr. Tomlinson, your words changed my life. Thank you!

For some students, science is easy. For some, it is hard; it was that way for me. If it had not been for my friends Jeff and Carmella, I never would have made it. To this day, I still don't understand what they saw in me, but, for whatever reason, they took me under their wings, and they taught me how to study and prepare for tests, and, most importantly, they taught me how to be a friend.

I know both Jeff and Carmella know just how much I appreciate them, but I never formally took the opportunity to tell them just how much their friendship meant to me. Without them, I never would have made it.

Jeff and Carmella, your friendship changed my life. I am forever grateful!

Dr. Patrick Leary was a professor of biology, a professor of the science of living things. Dr. Leary taught me about passion. I don't think I ever experienced a more passionate teacher. I don't believe I ever met anyone more enthused about their job or work than he was. He brought science to life. He brought life to science. It was magical!

There was something else he brought to life too. It was me. In a conversation, one day, he asked me why I had settled on becoming a nurse. When I explained and gave him my reasoning, he said he didn't understand why I was selling myself short on my abilities because he said he thought I would make a great doctor.

Even after I thoroughly explained why it would be impossible for me to go to medical school and become a physician, all he did was persist in telling me about how one of his other students had become a doctor at the age of 48. Dr. Leary saw something in me that I couldn't see in myself.

Dr. Leary, I will forever be grateful! Thank you!

Finally, I would be remiss if I didn't express my gratitude for Dr. Richard Logsdon, my English professor. English literature 101 is where I learned about writing and where I first learned that I actually had the potential to write well.

Like most students, my writing was fair, at best, but with Dr. Logsdon's guidance, and the gentle and persuasive power of his red pen, I learned what I needed to know to better communicate the ideas running around in my head.

Dr. Logsdon introduced me to the power of story, and he also introduced me to the work of Sylvia Plath. When I explained to him I had a dark story in me, he explained that even if I wrote about it, that didn't mean I ever had to share it with anyone and I found a tremendous amount of satisfaction in that. His words liberated me, and even though it has taken years to find my writing voice, I never forgot how he showed me that words had the potential to bring a story to life. After all these years, I have finally found my voice, and I am grateful I get to use it now to express my gratitude to Dr. Logsdon for planting a seed that took nearly three decades to grow.

Dr. Logsdon, I will be forever grateful. Thank you!

Gratitude is magic. Actually, gratitude is BIG magic. It has been and continues to be one of the guiding forces in my life. I am grateful for Big Inspirational Goals!

In Gratitude,

Bobby Kountz

MY MENTOR

by Marc Levine

One of my mentors is Tim Mulvaney. Tim founded a niche training company in NYC focused on diversity, inclusion, and courageous conversations. I worked for Tim for six years, selling and delivering training to hospitals, banks, and nonprofits in NYC.

Tim taught me to be courageous at the beginning of a new client project and discover "what's their greatest hope and what's their greatest fear."

The first time I heard this was after my first big sale. A hospital in Brooklyn, NY, hired us for a diversity training initiative. I was so proud and excited as we met with the six-member committee to begin planning this multi-month program.

The committee consisted of two members who weren't fans of ours. They voted against the project. Where I wanted to keep them at a distance, Tim was smart enough to invite them onto the planning committee. He was right. They shared their ideas and we listened; they became big fans and, eventually, proponents of extending our contract.

I was afraid to ask the committee members about their fears. "What if their fears are our fears?" I asked. I wanted to build momentum and positivity as we started. But Tim knew what Shrek confirms after he burps "better out than in."

Allowing everyone to voice their fears released the pressure. Their fears weren't underneath the surface clouding their judgment. They were out in the air. We could address their fears head on. We built credibility and connection. They thanked us for being caring enough to ask, and then listen.

I've used that model for the past fifteen years. I'm grateful to

Tim for teaching me to be courageous and give people a place to voice their fears.

THE BEST FRIEND WHO RAISED ME

by Glenna Gill

I'm not sure who was angrier that morning, me or my mother. For the last few months, I'd been spending the nights at various friends' houses so I didn't have to go home. Sometimes I'd call and let my mother know, but other times I'd conveniently forget and just show up at our apartment the next morning. This particular morning, my mother decided she'd had enough.

"Why don't you pack your stuff and go wherever it is you stay at night?"

Her words left me stunned. I was seventeen years old, still a minor. Where was I supposed to go? Pausing for a second, I realized the alternative was spending every night at home, a place where I never felt safe.

"Okay," I said in my calmest voice and headed to my room with a roll of garbage bags. Since I technically owned nothing besides my clothes and makeup, I was ready to leave in fifteen minutes with a trash bag in each hand.

"WAIT!" my mother shouted as I headed for the door. She tried to fake a smile, but I noticed the fear in her eyes much more. She thought I would cry and beg to stay.

"If you want to live here," my mother bargained, "a lot of things will have to change."

I was hoping she meant her new boyfriend, Glenn, who had parked himself on our couch six months ago and never left. We hardly ever spoke to each other, except when Glenn told dirty jokes that made me decidedly uncomfortable. My mother had met him in a mental health group in our city, and he'd been with us ever since. His mental illness was bipolar disorder. My mother had been diagnosed with everything under the sun, too much to make sense of for my seventeen-year-old brain.

My mother continued, "If you do all the dishes and make the beds every day and..."

I was no longer listening to her list of demands. For a brief moment, I saw freedom, and I wasn't about to let it slip out of my hands.

"No, Mom," I said as I exited the front door.

The first waves of panic from what I'd just done hit me while walking halfway up our street carrying my garbage bags. I was seventeen years old and homeless. My father couldn't take me in at the hotel where he worked and lived, so I didn't bother to ask him. It would have cost him his job to have me running around under his feet. The Florida heat was getting to its highest point of the day, but I kept walking and trying to think of a plan.

I ended up knocking on the door of the studio apartment where my friend Tim lived. He hugged me and let me in where he and several of our friends were eating McDonald's. My stomach rumbled as I realized I hadn't yet had breakfast or lunch. How would I be able to get enough food every day or a place to stay? I had a job at Sears, but it wasn't full-time or enough to support me. I concealed my hunger from my friends as I relayed the story of my mother kicking me out.

"I'm glad you left," Tim agreed. "Her boyfriend is pretty creepy. Why don't you just stay here?"

"For real?" My body instantly relaxed at his suggestion. I wouldn't have to sleep in the streets.

I took the twin bed on the other side of the small studio from where Tim slept. He made sure to include me in his dinner plans, so I was finally able to eat. It was embarrassing to be so needy, especially as Tim was only nineteen himself, but he never made me feel that way. He had his own car, so he let me tag along with him to flea markets and parties and anything else we came up with.

Tim encouraged me to save all the money I made at Sears so I could get a studio apartment of my own. He bought us groceries and wouldn't let me contribute to his rent. I stayed with him for about four months, and in all honesty, those are my best memories of being a teenager. Tim wasn't in love with me or I with him, but he made sure I was well taken care of and safe. When I finally got my own apartment, it was on the first floor right under his.

Now, nearly thirty years later, he is still one of my best friends. Sure, we've moved on and married people and had children, but it's never like any time has passed when I see him. He is still my hero as the young man who made my childhood happy despite all my family misery growing up.

Today, Tim is married to a wonderful woman and has a son going to middle school. He is one of the most spectacular fathers I've ever seen, but I never had any doubt.

MY PEOPLE

by Lorena Tovar

"What matters in life is not what happens to you but what you remember and how you remember it."
Gabriel Garcia Marquez

Today, at the age I am, I think about all the moments I have lived in every stage of my life. Looking back at the places where I lived, studied, worked, and looking around me, I feel calm, a great relief, happiness and gratitude for everything that God, life, and the universe has given me. Every year has brought wonderful people who have left a mark on my memories and in my heart. They have helped me to change my thoughts, my opinion, my personality, and my way of living.

I say thank you to my family (my mom, Amanda Tejada; my dad, Jorge Tovar, and my sister, Cristina Tovar), for being my strength of spirit, my pride and my true love. My mom is the most important woman in my life. Because of her, I am the woman I am. Although we have had disagreements and I have not been very open, she has always been loving and worried for us. She is kind hearted, patient, helpful, and loving, and she doesn't hold resentment in her soul. She believes in others when I'm not able to. She is confident when I am not. My mother teaches me many values and lessons every day, but the most significant one is the importance of spending time with family, helping and supporting each other. She has never been self-ish, she focuses on helping her siblings and her daughters, and she is true to her dreams.

In my childhood, I met great neighbors and wonderful people who took care of me and helped me grow up. I am very grateful to the Prieto family who invited me to their family parties where I met my childhood friends. With my friends; I laughed, I cried, and I fought, but always we made up. However, in time some of them moved away and I never saw them again, but there was one special person who remained a friend in my life. After all the years I've known her, she continues to surprise me because she always cares for her friends and thinks of others. She is always ready to listen without judgement. She is an honest, kind, understanding woman. I enjoy spending time with her. We go to church, cinemas, and restaurants on Sundays. Rocío Rodríguez, you have earned my admiration and respect because you are persistent, supportive, loyal, and loving. You have always been close to me, and you always walk with your friends.

When I was a student at the university and later as an employee, I have met many people for whom I am very grateful. They have been supportive, have helped me, and have given me their best. My friends from the university, Lady Vélez, Alexandra Manchola, and Ana María Hómez are exceptional. I am grateful for them because of our moments studying, dancing, at the "ferias," and all the experiences we have had together. Our group had the craziest women (Ana and Lady), a calm and prudent woman (Alexa), and one who fell down all the time (me) ... I still tumble, but I get up like nobody has seen it. I experienced many "first times" with these ladies: I drank to the point of intoxication, I visited many pubs and discos, I traveled and enjoyed "rock al parque" festival, etc. Thank you, my dear friends, for all the moments, for taking care of me, for all the gatherings, for being there for me, and for sharing special dates and special moments.

When I went to work in Quimbaya, Quindío, I remember my mother's aunt, Pobreza (R.I.P.). I stayed at her home. At the beginning I didn't feel comfortable, but after a few days I felt at home and I loved everything: her house, her animals, her kindness, and her delicious food. She was eighty, hard-working, and persistent. She kept an eye on every room of her house and treated me like a daughter. In my job, I met Estefania Ramos, a young woman with energy, vitality, a strong character, and many dreams. She was a great guide and a good friend. When I felt sad, she used to do things to change my mood. We would go to the gym, drink beer, walk, travel to Pereira, and have fun. I laughed a lot from her stories; we were confidantes. She was amazing. I learned to enjoy my job and make dreams come true.

When I began to work in Bogotá eight years ago, I made two beautiful friends. I never thought we would get along because we were so different, but surprisingly we became close and we would chat every day. I like the way they are: They are kind, funny, and friendly, and they have good hearts. Franci Arevalo is cheerful; she laughs all the time; her good mood is contagious; she is sensible and is a tidy woman; she loves her parents, siblings and nephews; she loves chocolates and dancing; when we get together, she is a very nice, understanding, tolerant, funny woman. Carolain Herrera is a woman who makes me laugh with her stories and her ideas; she is very sensitive; she has a beautiful soul; she is very charitable with people; she is always looking after us; she loves her family. We always travel in December and try to see each other every month.

Finally, these amazing people are special. I don't have words and actions to say thank you for everything. When I spend time with each one of them and their families, I feel at home as with my family; I feel comfortable. They give the best without expecting anything in return, and I appreciate it. They respect me as I am; I can rely on them, and they can rely on me.

To every single one, I say thank you for accepting me into your lives. I respect and admire you. I appreciate each one of you for being in my life. I enjoy each moment with you and the memories will remain always in my mind and in my heart.

Lorena Tovar

LEADERS MATTER

by Alise Cortez

Dr. Alise Cortez is the chief purpose officer at Alise Cortez and Associates and chief ignition officer at Gusto, Now! She is also an inspirational speaker, social scientist, author, and host of the Working on Purpose radio show.

I grew up in a small town in northeastern Oregon with a population of 4,800. My strongest aspiration my senior year of high school was to find a way to get out. Little did I know my ticket would come through the co-op work project. That's where I met Roland Haertl, who owned the pump company I briefly worked at for the co-op assignment. After a few telephone exchanges as he called into the office to speak to various personnel, one day he said something that was the beginning of changing my life forever: He told me I had a job in Portland if I ever found myself in the city. And there it was – my ticket out!

I took him up on that offer. After graduating high school, I moved to Portland some 160 miles west and earned a diploma from a business college, where I attended classes for eight months. Afterwards, I promptly went to work for Roland as his administrative assistant in the small commercial real estate firm he owned. It was incredible to work for this man! He taught me so much about life and business, and he was always jovial and fun, ever optimistic.

One day, 18 months into the job, on his way out for lunch, he strode past me sitting in the reception area. He opened the door out to the hallway, and called over his shoulder: "You've got to get out of here, see the world, get an education, but before you go, hire your replacement." Wham, the door slammed shut behind him.

I sat bewildered, wondering what had just transpired, never moving from my frozen perch at my typewriter. Repeatedly, I asked myself, "Did he just fire me?" A little over an hour later, that same door opened, and Roland strode through it and cheerfully headed back to his office. Stopping him in his tracks, I asked, "Did you just fire me?" Cheerfully and with an arresting directness, he replied, "Absolutely, it would be a crime to keep you here."

Before Roland uttered this famous termination sentence, I did not know I could attend college. It never occurred to me. My parents were successful entrepreneurs – we never talked about college, ever. A Bachelors, two Masters, and a PhD later, I think I can check the education box. I would soon move to Madrid, Spain, where I lived for six months, learned Spanish well (having already learned French), and traveled all over Western Europe. What an incredibly enriching experience for this small-town Oregonian girl. I then moved to Rio de Janeiro, Brazil, for two years, where I learned Portuguese and traveled all over South America. I've since delivered programs and spoken across the world. So I think I'm progressing well on the travel front – and I've got a hunger to continue. Now, that bit about doing something with my life, that path continues as I unfold further onto my journey as a management consultant specializing in meaning and purpose, inspirational speaker, author, and radio show host.

The gift of Roland's utterance represented pure possibility. He opened the door so big to what my life could be – I could never have imagined for myself the picture he painted for me. In every way, he saved me. Saved me from living a much smaller life. Saved me from limiting my potential. Saved me by leading me to what I could become.

I am eternally grateful to this man. I recognized him at my wedding in 2000, alongside my parents, for his contribution to my life. Most years since, I've met him for lunch during my trek back to Portland from Dallas, where I live today. I tell him how much he has radically altered my life for the better and how I appreciate his role in my life and absolutely love him for it. When I went through my divorce in early 2016, Roland called me every weekend to check on my emotional and spiritual well-being. Together in the summer of 2015 we'd hatched a plan to celebrate his 80th birthday, in the form of a "living wake," as he did not want to have to die to know how people felt about him. How glorious it was to help facilitate the celebration of his life and the myriad ways he touched so many.

Roland has shown me how to be an inspirational leader, and now I help develop them in companies across the world. He believed in me in a way no one had before, or perhaps has since. My life is infinitely enriched because this man sprung me out of the small town I grew up in, fired me from a job I loved, and ignited a flame in me to become everything I can in my life. As I write these words, tears stream down my cheeks. Still, after all these 35 years, his gift to my life moves me to tears.

A TRADITION

by Peter B Willliams

Peter B. Williams is the author of Productive Accidents — *a playbook for personal and professional adventure. He is a speaker, serial volunteer, and board member at Music For Life International, and Resolve Foundation*

I grew up on the outskirts of Armidale, New South Wales, a rural town on the eastern edge of Australia. Our neighbours, Mr. and Mrs. Clark, were such excellent gardeners that they had extended their vegetable patch across their entire lawn, over the front fence, all the way to the dirt road that separated our properties.

Late one afternoon in November 1978, my older brother, Matthew, and I decided to race our pre-BMX bikes (they were heavy with full-suspension, designed to mimic motocross motorcycles) down this dirt road toward the gate that led to our home. We pedalled up the bumpy road to start the race, toward the highway that bordered the family farm machinery business, founded by our parents only six years earlier.

Not surprisingly, Matthew beat me in the first race, but it wasn't clear to me if the result was because he was bigger or better, or due to different bikes — his bike was newer and lighter. So we switched bikes to test the theory. Taking off in the second race, I was determined to keep pedalling the entire way, including over all the corrugated bumps of hard clay that had formed on the dirt road from wheels and rain over the years.

Suddenly the chain bounced off the front sprocket, leaving my legs spinning in thin air. Worse, it meant that the only way to stop the bike was no longer available. Back pedal brakes only work if the chain connects the front and rear sprocket, so I had a split second to make a terrifying choice — crash the bike for certain pain, or continue beyond our driveway and attempt to ride down the steep gully, into a twisted series of single track trails, used for moving cattle between nearby properties.

I knew this trail as well as an eight year old can know anything (although we had only lived at that address for the past two years, so maybe my mind is mixing the memories that formed later). So I decided to ride down the steep gully, hoping to make it to the flat section and roll to a safe stop. First I had to dodge the twenty-metre-tall telegraph poles that lay ready to be installed on the edge of the road, choosing to hug the barbed wire fence on the left, then to quickly switch to the right at the base of the gully, aiming for a wider and safer section of track. But there were so many pebbles that my wheels washed out, sending me through a blackberry bush, headfirst through the thorns, into a hidden tree stump — in the days before helmets.

Mr. Clark was in his front yard tending his pumpkins and other produce that spilled toward the road. He had heard the sudden scream and seen the bike disappear down the track. He was the first to rush down and find my mangled mess, shouting back up the hill for someone to call an ambulance.

Two weeks later, I returned home from hospital. There was some intensive care and surgery to fix a fractured jaw or skull.. and plenty of stitches, above my left eye, and some that dissolved in my mouth. It was near the end of the school year with not long before holidays. I rested at home those couple of weeks, but soon took an opportunity to work for Mr. and Mrs. Clark, helping to pick cherries down the hill, in an orchard next to that tree stump.

At $1 per bucket, I was able to earn eight dollars a day, amassing $40 by the end of the first week, enabling me to buy my first skateboard — an orange fibreglass weapon with red wheels for $20. I'm sure my parents were thrilled with the purchase.

Mr. Clark was born exactly fifty years prior to me. If he were still alive he would be turning one hundred on the ninth of the ninth, twenty twenty. So this letter is a thank you to Mr. and Mrs. Clark for calling the ambulance, my first job, that skateboard, and for all the birthday cake over the years. It's also a reminder for me to keep a lookout for any friends or neighbours that give birth to a child on 9.9.2020 — to keep the 50 year tradition alive.

Peter B. Williams - Hong Kong - September 2020

FROM BACKSTAGE TO ONSTAGE

by Todd Cherches

Todd Cherches is the CEO of NYC-based executive coaching firm BigBlueGumball, an Adjunct Professor of leadership at NYU and Columbia University, and the author of "VisuaLeadership: Leveraging the Power of Visual Thinking in Leadership and in Life."

My entire life, from grade school through graduate school and well into my thirties, I was, by nature, what I call a "3 B's" kind of guy: a Back-of-the-Room, Behind-the-Scenes, Bookworm.

An extreme introvert with social anxiety disorder, I was most comfortable and most productive when working in solitude. I was fine occasionally interacting with people one-on-one or in small groups if I knew and trusted everyone (and if I felt what is now commonly referred to as "psychological safety"). But I was not the type to speak up in meetings; and when it came to public speaking in front of a room, I was both absolutely terrified of it and completely terrible at it.

So…how did I go from being "that guy" to, just a few years later, a leadership trainer and executive coach, the CEO of my own consulting firm, a three-time award-winning adjunct professor at NYU, a lecturer at Columbia University, a TEDx speaker, a published author, and a professional public speaker?

Back when I was 34, after ten years of trying to make it in Hollywood as a studio executive, but not getting anywhere (primarily due to my lack of experience and confidence), I eventually gave up and moved back home to New York City.

With no job prospects and no idea what I was going to do with my career, after months of one failed job interview after another, I finally ended up getting hired as a program manager by an industry-leading management training company, where I was put in charge of revamping their mini-MBA program. I didn't have any experience at all in this area, but they hired me based on my L.A. project management experience even though, as a former English literature major, the only thing I knew about an "MBA" was how to spell it.

Leveraging what little business experience I had, I dove headfirst into learning everything I could about management and leadership by reading one book after another and observing the company's management trainers in action. I would sit way in the back of the training room and watch in awe of their knowledge and their ability, as well as their confidence. "Wow...I could never in a million years envision myself being up there doing anything like that!" I would think to myself...with just a little bit of envy. But I was more than content being the behind-the-scenes, back-of-the-room bookworm that I always was and was always destined to be.

Until one day...

I was asked by my boss to fill in for another program manager and oversee a three-day "Leadership Program for Presidents" down at a luxury golf resort in Hilton Head, SC. I was more than a little nervous, as this was going to be a workshop for a group of 12 small-company CEOs, a group much more senior than I was used to being around. But I knew, liked, and trusted the trainer, Alex Johnson, whom I had worked with many times before, so, despite being a little more nervous than usual, I flew down to Hilton Head the evening before the start of the workshop so that I could review the content and materials that night, and then get everything all set up early the next morning so that it was all good-to-go for the trainer to just walk in and get started.

Only things were not good-to-go when I woke up at 7:00am that next morning, as there was a message for me on the hotel answering machine (*this was in the days before cell phones) from Alex the trainer saying that he got really sick with food poisoning the night before, woke up late, and missed his flight. He would not be able to get there until later than evening...if at all. And, again, this was Day One of a three-day program.

What to do?

In a panic I called my boss back in New York (who I didn't like, trust, or get along with, by the way), and he said to me that we have only two options: One, we cancel the program, have to refund everyone's money (including all their travel expenses!), and have a group of twelve really disappointed and angry CEO-level clients on our hands. Or, he said, "The only other choice is YOU facilitate the training." Um...excuse me...what? Here I was, never having spoken in front of people before, and I was now being asked to get up there and facilitate a leadership training program for twelve CEOs??? This group was going to be expecting a seasoned, well-known, 60-year-old management consultant to be their facilitator...and they were going to end up with some unknown and untested 34-year-old guy who didn't have any idea what he was doing...or how to do it?

As my boss wished me good luck, his last words to me were: "They are expecting Alex, and they are getting you. So make sure you do a great job...and whatever you do, do NOT let them know that you've never done this before! I do NOT want an angry mob on my hands or anyone calling me demanding a refund!"

So, with no other option, and gathering up all the fake confidence, energy, and extroversion I could muster, I proceeded to greet each CEO upon their arrival, asked them to take their seats, and meekly announced, "Hi, my name is Todd. Welcome to the program."

I had two options at this point: Do I fake my way through it as if I knew what I was doing (as my boss had demanded) and hope that no one notices? Or should I be candid with them, explain the situation honestly, and see how they react? Well, instead of taking my boss's advice, I took mine. And I am so glad that I did! For, instead of having a mutiny on my hands, these CEOs, twelve complete strangers up until just a few moments ago, banded together to say, "Gentlemen…how are we going to get our young friend, Todd, here, through this little dilemma?"

Wow. Instead of beating me up, these twelve incredible leaders selflessly banded together to lift me up. They were all there to learn about leadership, but through their empathetic, compassionate, and caring words and actions, they taught me, and one another, more about what true leadership looks like than the originally-planned version of this workshop ever would have.

When I got back to my hotel room after that first day, as they all went off to play golf and have dinner together, there was a message from the trainer, Alex: He was feeling better and would be arriving later that evening, ready to take over on the morning of Day Two.

Amazingly, rather than feeling relieved, I actually felt somewhat disappointed. I had realized that day that when it came to getting up in front of a room, I wasn't really as terrible at it as I would have thought, nor was I as terrified of it as I might have expected. In fact, if I'm being completely honest, it was actually kind of fun. Over the course of that first day, that training room became a new extension of my comfort zone. And I had a realization that, hey, I could actually do this if I had to… or if I ever wanted to. While I was far from great at it, being good at it was no longer that far removed from who I was…or who I could, potentially, be.

And while it would be three years before I would take my next steps forward towards becoming the confident, professional public speaker that I am today (*despite my still being that same extreme introvert deep inside!), that summer day in Hilton Head was a turning point for me that changed everything forever. And although the names of those twelve CEOs are long forgotten, their impact and influence on me all these years later will always be remembered. And, for that, I will remain eternally grateful.

by Madeline Haslam

Madeline Haslam is the research coordinator at 7:47 Club

Throughout our career, we have sparked over 500,000 relationships through in-person and virtual Gratitude Experiences. At the heart of these Gratitude Experiences is our gratitude question, which asks, "If you could give credit or thanks to one person in your life who you don't give enough credit or thanks to, who would that be?" Our signature gratitude question essentially does one of two things. It allows any darkness of the past to be brought into the light, or it helps us see the light from our past and appreciate it in the present. Our gratitude question helps our attendees open their minds and cultivate initial connections as well as their own feelings on those who have influentially shaped their lives. Our 7:47 Gratitude Experience was created because we know how it feels to be isolated, lonely, and disconnected and to crave a way to make meaningful human connections. Early on, we learned that just because things may look good on paper does not mean they feel good in the heart. Success is not significant if it leaves you unfulfilled.

Our founder, Chris Schembra, knows this all too well. 7:47's journey began in the early summer of 2015. Chris had just returned home to New York City after producing a Broadway play in Italy. Feeling disconnected from his work and a sense of isolation upon returning, he began to experiment with some dishes in his kitchen and accidentally created a revolutionary pasta sauce recipe. Chris knew he needed an outside opinion on his sauce recipe. On July 15th, 2015, he invited 15 of his friends over for dinner and served them his new pasta sauce. Not only did they enjoy the meal, but they liked the structure of the dinner, filled with delegated tasks, shared activities, and communal discussion. Chris fell in love with the joy of connecting people. And the experiences went on to save his life.

How do we ask the gratitude question?

How we ask our signature gratitude question changes slightly based on whether our 7:47 Gratitude Experience is in-person or virtual. For in-person experiences, the gratitude question is asked around the dinner table where attendees share with the person next to them. I'll focus solely on explaining our virtual Gratitude Experiences here since they have been our preferred mode of connection since the pandemic.

During our virtual Gratitude Experiences, the gratitude question is asked in the second-act of our three-act "play." It is useful to conceptualize our virtual Gratitude Experiences as a three-act play. The first act is a pause to connect into the present through emotions and mindful sharing. The second act is a dive into the past using our signature gratitude question. And the third act is a look-ahead to the future using shared values. The second act begins with a lesson on listening and asking questions with a posture of openness. Following this mini-lesson, we ask our signature gratitude question, "If you could give credit or thanks to one person in your life who you don't give enough credit or thanks to, who would that be?" Attendees are then split up into break-out groups of three for 15 minutes to share an answer to the question. These small breakout groups allow for a more intimate, safe space for our attendees to open their minds, ask guiding questions, and flourish with a sense of gratitude while they answer. When the 15 minutes are up, a facilitated discussion unfolds in the main Zoom room, where people talk about the gratitude stories shared in their breakout group.

What happens when we ask the gratitude question?

Simply put, our gratitude question leads to massive, transformative life changes. We have gathered data from over 90 Gratitude Experiences, and with that data, we have learned how our attendees change emotionally from our Gratitude Experiences. At the start of our Gratitude Experiences, our attendees' top three emotions are tired, excited, and anxious. At the end of our Gratitude Experiences, the top three emotions said are connected, grateful, and happy. While there is tremendous value in this qualitative data, merely knowing the top emotions said is not enough. We have taken all of the emotions that have ever been said at our Gratitude Experiences and put them on a numerical scale. We had multiple judges rank them on a scale from one to five, with one being very negative, three being neutral, and five being very positive. We then took the ranked emotions and analyzed how the emotions change from the start of a Gratitude Experience to the end. And the results are incredible!

At the start of an average Gratitude Experience, attendees are emotionally at a 2.75 out of 5 with a standard deviation of 1.61. This means that our typical attendee is coming in feeling negative, below the neutral threshold, with much variance in the spectrum of feelings, as demonstrated by the high standard deviation. After we ask our signature gratitude question that 2.75 changes to a 4.49 out of 5 with a standard deviation of 0.64. That is a 1.74 increase on a 5-point scale of emotions with a tighter clustering around that average. These results support the positive transformational effect of our 7:47 Gratitude Experiences. People start out feeling rather negative, pretty scattered, but shift to feeling extremely positive and more closely aligned with one another by the end.

What the gratitude question is essentially doing is taking the fire that is external in our lives and kindling it internally. We help create a fire within our attendees. We ignite an initial spark with our gratitude question, and throughout our 7:47 Gratitude Experience, it grows into a fire. This fire we help our attendees build continues to spread for some time after the Gratitude Experience. But every fire needs fuel, so our attendees are encouraged to develop some kind of maintenance to keep that fire burning (i.e., 7:47 coaching or 7:47 Gratitude Experiences).

Attendees are building and strengthening their social connections with other attendees and those that people gave gratitude towards. When the Gratitude Experience is over, and you go out and thank the person you gave credit and thanks to, that relationship is also strengthened. Once an initial spark is put back in a relationship, it will keep growing because that is what gratitude is. It creates that positive upward momentum, that fire within. If you're looking to connect more with your team, clients, family, friends, or even strangers, if you crave connection, real, genuine human connection, our 7:47 Gratitude Experience is how you spark it. With the initial sharing, the meeting, the openness, the questions, and facilitation, we hit it all. It is not just a simple gratitude activity. It is sharing, analyzing, thinking, reframing, and shifting perspectives. It is transformative in a single word, and if you make it a habit, it will change your life forever. We inspire action in our attendees through gratitude, and this action takes form in many different shapes and sizes. It can look like changing your career, working on a new project with a coworker, moving to a new city, reaching out to a long-lost friend or family member, or revealing your true identity and becoming the person you have always longed to be. Whatever the action is that you're desiring to take, don't wait around for motivation to hit you. Forge ahead yourself with gratitude as your guide.

LOVE BOMB

by Mark Shapiro

Mark Shapiro, founder of the LoveBomb app, is at the forefront of social innovation. He's given the premiere TEDx talk on human connection in the digital age and has been featured on CBS, The School of Greatness Podcast, Thrive Global, and Educate Inspire Change.

After my dad passed away, I realized I could show more appreciation for the people in my life and started a daily ritual of sending personalized video messages to each of my 3,000 Facebook friends on their birthdays.

While I guessed it would be a nice gift to give and help me keep in touch, little did I know that sending appreciation videos would totally elevate my life, strengthen my relationships, and be a gift that keeps on giving.

To give it a bit of scope, I've always been a very social person but had a long standing tendency of falling out of touch with people that were important to me, I gave social media too much control over my social life and who I engaged with, and I lacked confidence in myself and my relationships.

I was the kind of guy that wouldn't post on social media in fear of being judged, didn't reach out to people out of fear of rejection, and would often tell people what I thought they wanted to hear instead of what was true and authentic for me.

So you can imagine how much of a stretch it was for me to go from the super self-conscious guy to the person who sends personalized video messages to everyone he knows. But I did it anyway, and it very quickly became my most cherished and most consistent daily ritual (perhaps even more-so than showering and my morning cup of coffee).

You see, gratitude and kindness are proven to stimulate positive emotions, improve our health, and help build strong relationships. Also, they are contagious, so giving someone our kind attention (even if it's just a 30-second appreciation video or a 'thinking of you' text) is often a bigger gift than we realize.

Everyone feels socially isolated at times (especially amidst a global pandemic), so any touch points that influence more love and less disconnect are an amazing gift.

Needless to say, the messages consistently blow people away and really stand out from a generic/impersonal "happy birthday" Facebook wall post.

From my experience, here's what makes an awesome appreciation or birthday video:

-A warm smiley face…

-Saying where you are and what you are up to (to create some connection). Bonus points for sending from some place cool, like an exotic location or in front of a historical/recognizable landmark.

-Paying an honest compliment or recalling a memory, then wishing them well.

-Making it short and sweet, 20-40 seconds for most contacts. Don't ramble.

-Don't ask for anything in return, make it too much about you, or say anything you don't mean.

My favorite thing to say is: "Whatever your birthday wish is today, I'm sending good vibes your way for it to come true."

As of today, four years after starting this ritual, I've sent over 10,000 personalized birthday videos (reaching all 3,000 of my Facebook friends once per year). It equates to 8 per day and takes no more than 10 minutes per day.

People consistently tell me how much of an impact the message made, or that they had been looking forward to receiving the message all day. About once a week, someone tells me that they started sending birthday videos, or they share with me a story of an interaction they had with someone (that was inspired by my video to them and wouldn't have happened without it). One person even told their dad they love him for the first time, so clearly there is so much more love to go around and so many kind words and authentic feelings that are currently being left unexpressed.

This is a shame for both the potential giver and receiver because it robs both people an incredible opportunity for meaningful connection. Needless to say, there are no guarantees in life, so it's important that we acknowledge the people we care about today and before it's too late.

While expressing our feelings towards others can be challenging or awkward at first, it's a muscle that can be strengthened with practice. When I got started, I was a novice: I was uncomfortable and awkward. But like any habit growth, I've gotten better and know that it's about gratitude, giving, and sharing good vibes, more than it is getting the words exactly right.

Here's why I still send daily LoveBombs and why I recommend it to anybody!

Benefits of loving kindness:

-Increases happiness and confidence

-Decreases anxiety and depression

-Deepens connection

-Attracts more good into your life

-Instantly makes the world a brighter place

Sending the birthday videos is a gratitude practice that reminds me who I am and what I stand for everyday, which feels amazing and always brightens up a dark day.

It's opened up amazing opportunities in my life, like speaking on the TEDx stage, a myriad of business opportunities, hundreds of party invites/social plans, TV news interviews, the creation of the LoveBomb app, and I'm contributing to this awesome new book!

It's also made me see how much more kindness and connection is available in the world.

We all love to get genuine attention from someone because we want to know who cares and why and need the reminder as we go about our busy, stressful, and sometimes isolated lives. As a result, we have nothing to lose by reaching out to someone, reminding them of our past exchanges/the value/imprint they've had in our life, and by encouraging them forward. It will make us feel great, it will make them feel great, and we'll be so glad we did it!

BIO

Chris Palmore is a gratitude conductor, coach, creator, and author. He is the founder of GratitudeSpace and a host on GratitudeSpace Radio. He has a Media And Performing Arts Degree and a minor in Video and Broadcasting from Savannah College of Art and Design and is a proud member of The International Alliance of Theater and Stage Employees (I.A.T.S.E.). He lives with his wife, Rocío, in Louisville, KY.

A PARTING REQUEST

GratitudeSpace's sole purpose is to be a catalyst for gratitude. If you want to contribute in any way, then I'd love to connect with you.

If this book has inspired you to connect with another or write a letter of gratitude, I'd love to hear from you. I'm going to collect these essays and letters and compile another book filled with the gratitude that has been inspired directly from this book. People sharing gratitude inspire others to share gratitude and the circle continues, and this book will create another book. It just takes a person to decide to take action and connect their gratitude with its rightful owner.

When this happens, if you'd like to share the story or letter you wrote, I want to read it. Go here to share and submit: www.gratitudespace.com/deargratitude.

In Gratitude,
Chris Palmore

GRATITUDE CHECKLIST

This section is no small feat for a book about gratitude. As much as I'd like to tell the story of all those whom I am grateful for, I just can't because that would take a whole book. This is a problem I am humbly grateful for.

My gratitude team helped to take my hopes and dreams and make them a reality. I can not thank you all enough but will continually try to!

Thomas Koulopoulos

Noosha Ravaghi

Bobby Kountz

I'd like to acknowledge my gratitude for all who have contributed to this book:

A. Allan (page 233)
Girma Bishaw (page 96)
Gail Boenning (pages 92, 205)
Kate Boston (page 40)
Adrienne Brown (page 108)
Richard Calautti (page 20)
Kevin Caldwell (page 59)
Carmin Caterina (page 130)
Warisara Changkaew (page 151)
Todd Cherches (page 261)
Beth & Pete Christianson (page 157)
Alise Cortez (page 255)
Nicola Davies (page 64)
Shawn Davis (page 113)
Chris Davis (page 241)
Elena Giacomin Dennis (page 158)
Tiffany Dennis (page 159)
Teddy Droseros (page 243)
Edinho (page 221)
Ifumi Ehigiator (pages 139, 235)
Barbara Faison (page 175)
Farhana (page 34)
Bobsy Gaia (page 62)
Glenna Gill (page 249)
Krystle Gossett (page 148)
Elizabeth Hartigan (page 210)
Madeline Haslam (page 265)
Elizabeth Holland (page 81)
Lina Isabel (page 188)

A.J. Jacobs (page 125)
JessMag (page 180)
Medea Kalantar (page 231)
Bobby Kountz (pages 177, 236, 244)
Erica Ladden (page 150)
Tanya Ladden (page 152)
Jeannie Ladden (page 153)
Nancy Liu Lan (page 239)
Marc Levine (pages 176, 234, 247)
Mollie McGlocklin (page 48)
Parker McGuffey (page 185)
Tammy Meyers (page 154)
Sasha Michael (page 140)
Brandy M. Miller (page 128)
Danielle Moody (page 69)
Sha Nacino (page 73)
Michael O'Brien (page 56)
Al Palmore (page 219)
Nika Paradis (page 229)
Janhvi Parmar (page 170)
Tonya Patterson (page 161)
Abbie Pierce (page 60)
Elizabeth de la Portilla (page 133)
Hillis Pugh (page 114)
Rocío Del Mar Rodríguez Pulido (pages 165, 192, 213)
Noosha Ravaghi (pages 102, 208)
Diane Riley (pages 86, 136)
Karen Roach (page 156)
Catherine Robertson (page 44)
Hilary Russo (page 217)
Ava Safran (page 67)
Mark Shapiro (page 269)

Aeon Solo (page 172)

Wally Stewart (page 163)

Lorena Tovar (page 252)

Viko (pages 76, 183)

Isabella Williams (page 71)

Peter B. Willliams (page 258)

I'm grateful for all the people I've had the pleasure to meet during the Punching Depression Tour, interact with for GratitudeSpace, and interview on GratitudeSpace Radio. If I hadn't worked with these grateful souls, I would have never felt motivated to work on an anthology about gratitude:

Allyson Akers
Maddie-Jo Anderson
Shawn Anderson
Dave Asprey
Ben Avanzato
Giovanni Axibal
Daniel (Shanti) Banfai
Chriselda Barretto
Georgian Benta
Girma Bishaw
Gail Boenning
Corey Boston
Paul Boynton
Devin Brown
Daniel (Danno) Burrow
Willie Burton
Vernetta Cail
Kevin Caldwell
Adam Carolla
Ronnie Caswell
Carmin Caterina
Todd Cherches
Kevin Christensen
Erik Christopher
Adam Clayton
Curtis Cockrell
Kim Cole

Dr. Alise Cortez
Joe Cross
Shawn Davis
Deemah Dee
Tiffany Dennis
Mark Dhamma
Dieseldonlow
Emma Dilemma
Teddy Droseros
Prince Ea
Luke Earthwalker
Leticia Estrada
Mordecai Cohen Ettinger
Dave Evans
Tim Ferriss
Justin (Koko) Fowler
Ron Fowler
Neal Francis
Shannon Franklin
Tara Frost
Alex Gambino
Elisabeth Gambino
Joel Gerdis
Nathan Goetz
Krystle Gossett
Kevin Grangier
Rachel Greco
Tom Green
Brian Grubba
Richard Hallmarq
Brent Harrod
Janell Hartman
Paul Hewson

Megan Hills
Liz Holland
Susan Houck
Lewis Howes
Jonathan Isaacs
Samuel J
A.J. Jacobs
Doc Jen
Dan Johnson
Medea Kalantar
Florian Karl
Dashama Konah
Nikita Krivoshey
Greg Ladden
Erica Ladden
Steve Ladden
Megan Lawing
Laura Lebron
Melanie Levi
Marc Levine
Audrey Lin
Anthony Lee Lowe
Cristiane Machado
Jack Mackenroth
Oksana Makarova
Dimitri Makarova
Bill McGee
Caitlin McGrath
Sharon McPeake
Nav Menon
Brandy Miller
Adam Miramon
Carlos Mitchell

Larry Mullen Jr.
Sha Nancio
Michael O'Brien
Ryan Ong Palao
JacQi Marie Patterson
Emily Payne
Jefreux Peairs
Matt Perraut
Jade Piña
Shaun Michael Quick
Albert Recinos
Edward Alan Reed II
Bryan Reeves
Mark Reklau
Annie Rettic
Fred Reyes
Cheryl Rice
Catherine Robertson
Wietske Rubow
Hilary Russo
Jenny Santi
Lotan Sapir
Manu Satsangi
Chris Schembra
Josh Schwartz
Justin Sebastian
Rajesh Setty
Parul Sharma
Lindsey Shaw
Steven Sieden
Tracy Skinner
Stefanie Skupin
Ralph Smart

Melissa Smith
Jerry Springer
Anthony Stagg
Shawn Stevenson
Deano Sutter
Julie Thompson
Thor
John Torma
Chantal Van Rooyen
Kim Vandenberg
Antonio Vereen
Kerri Verna
Victor Vulovic
Matt Wheaton
Peter B. Williams
Anne Wong
Chris Wynn
Patrick Xu
"Weird Al" Yankovic
Gino Yu
Marianne Zickuhr

The Sisters of Perpetual Indulgence
    I'm grateful to...

Velveeta VonTease for your friendship and for connecting me with all of the sisters. The amount of gratitude that has been sparked from meeting you is overwhelming.

Sister Agatha Frisky for taking GratitudeSpace to Ybor City.

Sister Unity for our time on Hollywood Blvd and that beautiful afternoon.

Sister Roma for showing me all the gratitude the Castro District had to offer and more!

Sister Loosy hands up the best gratitude wing-nun in the business!

Sister Electra-Complex for our time in Laguna and those surprise gratitude videos that came across the wire from your students.

Sister Lotti Da for the Gratitude Crawl back in 2016 and adding just the right amount of sparkle and glitter needed to Gratitude New York!

Podcasters that have allowed me to share my gratitude story on:

Georgian Benta - The Gratitude Podcast

Shawn and Jen Davis - Hope Radio Podcast

Michael Roderick - Access to Anyone Podcast

Michael O'Brien - The Kintsugi Podcast

Tammy Gooler Loeb - Work from the Inside Out

Hilary Russo - HIListically Speaking

I want to give special thanks to:

Corey Boston, my best and oldest friend, for all the adventures and always being a beacon for understanding, thoughtfulness, and laughter;

Rick Schirmer, my gratitude brother, oldest friend, and mentor;

Dr. Patrick Williams, for being the calm in the storm and the best person to care for not only my mom but my dad, sister, and me;

Paul Boynton, for your grateful heart and openness to share it with me;

Grandma, Verla Gates, for loving me and always holding a space of presence whenever we were together... I miss you but know that love doesn't end once a person passes;

Chris Schembra, for your willingness to be a part of this book, the gratitude experiences, and grateful connections;

Peter B. Williams, for the Productive Accidents Series, your friendship, and all the excitement;

Curtis Cockrell, for the Gratitude and Sobriety Series, your strength in sobriety, family, and friendship;

and last but not least,

Rocío, not only for assisting me with the translation of the Spanish submissions, but also for grounding me, inspiring me, being my partner in adventure, and my wonderful coincidence.

As someone who practices the art of gratitude squared and gratitude cubed, I want to thank some of the people whose work has contributed to my gratitude journey and this book.

I want to thank Bill Gates for pioneering the personal computer and Steve Jobs for being the driving force behind the laptop that was used to write this book. I want to thank Jeff Bezos for the platform that I will be publishing and selling this on. I want to thank Brad West and Brad Andalman for the Vellum ebook creating software. I want to thank Evan Williams for creating Google Blogger which helped me find some of the writers who contributed to this anthology. I want to thank Mark Zuckerberg for Facebook, Jack Dorsey, Noah Glass, Evan Williams, and Biz Stone for Twitter, Kevin Systrom for Instagram, and Jawed Karim, Chad Hurley, and Steve Chen for YouTube; these platforms have allowed me to connect with others and share gratitude in ways that would have otherwise been impossible. I want to thank Reid Hoffman, Konstantin Guericke, Allen Blue, Jean-Luc Vailiant, and Eric Ly for creating LinkedIn and allowing me another way to connect with grateful people. I want to thank Brian Acton and Jan Koum for creating the ultimate free messaging, conversation, and video communication tool WhatsApp. I want to thank Larry Page and Sergey Brin for Google Drive and Gmail, which were used daily in the creation of this book. Lastly, I'd like to thank Keith Blount for creating Scrivener.

Made in the USA
Monee, IL
19 January 2021